arihant
SUCCESS AND NOTHING LESS

Be a TOP SCORER in ICSE Exams 2025

i Succeed

10 Sample Question Papers

with Quick Study Notes

English Language 10th

Paper 1

AUTHORS
Vaishali Jaiswal
Pramila Agarwal

Arihant Prakashan
(School Division Series)

Administrative & Production Offices

Regd. Office
'Ramchhaya' 4577/15, Agarwal Road, Darya Ganj, New Delhi -110002
Tele: 011- 47630600, 43518550

Head Office
Kalindi, TP Nagar, Meerut (UP) - 250002
Tel: 0121-7156203, 7156204

Sales & Support Offices
Agra, Ahmedabad, Bengaluru, Bareilly, Chennai, Delhi, Guwahati, Hyderabad, Jaipur, Jhansi, Kolkata, Lucknow, Nagpur & Pune.

PRICE ₹165.00

PO No : TXT-XX-XXXXXXX-X-XX

Published by Arihant Publications (India) Ltd.

For further information about the books published by Arihant, log on to www.arihantbooks.com or e-mail at info@arihantbooks.com

Follow us on

i Succeed

SAMPLE QUESTION PAPERS

THE **BEST CHOICE** OF TEACHERS & STUDENTS, Why?

01 Exact Exam Pattern

All Sample Papers have been designed on the actual exam format of ICSE

02 Complete Syllabus

Complete coverage of syllabus through different types of questions across all the sample papers

03 Latest Specimen Question Paper

Latest Specimen Question Paper with detailed answers.

04 Detailed Answers

Step-by-step answers to help you understand concepts and improve problem-solving skills.

05 All Type of Questions

Coverage of all type of exam pattern questions, writing task, grammar & reading comprehension.

Free Doubt Solving APP

To help you sort out your doubts at any time any place.

i Succeed

English Language 10

PREPARATION ASSESSMENT ZONE 1-21

PROFICIENCY BUILDING ZONE 23-106

Course Structure
2024-25

There will be one paper of two hours duration of 80 marks and Internal Assessment of practical work carrying 20 marks.

There will be one paper of two hours duration carrying 80 marks and Internal Assessment of 20 marks. In paper, total Five questions will be set and all of which will be compulsory.

PAPER I: THEORY **80 Marks**

Question 1 : Candidates will be required to write a composition of about 300–350 words from a choice of subjects which will test their ability to: organise, describe, narrate, report, explain, persuade or argue, present ideas coherently with accuracy and precision, compare and contrast ideas and arrive at conclusions, present relevant arguments and use correct style and format.

The topic will be varied and may be suggested by language or by other stimuli such as pictures. The topics will be so chosen so as to allow the candidates to draw on first-hand experience or to stimulate their imagination.

The organisation of subject matter, syntax, punctuation, correctness of grammatical constructions and spelling will be expected to be appropriate to the mode of treatment required by the subject.

Question 2 : Candidates will have to write a letter from a choice of two subjects requiring either a formal or an informal mode of treatment. Suggestions regarding the content of the letter may be given. The format of the letter with address, introduction, conclusion, etc., will form part of the assessment. Special attention must be paid to the format of the letter with emphasis on vocabulary appropriate to the context.

Question 3 : Candidates will be given a specific situation and will be required to:

(a) Write the text for a notice based on given directions.

(b) Write an e-mail on the same content as the notice.

Question 4 : An unseen prose passage of about 500 words will be given. Uncommon items of vocabulary, or structure will be avoided. A question will be set to test vocabulary. Candidates will be required to show an understanding of the words/phrases in the context in which they have been used.

A number of questions requiring short answers will also be asked on the passage. These questions will test the candidates' ability to comprehend the explicit content and organisation of the passage and to infer information, intention and attitude from it.

The last question will consist of a summary that will test the candidates' ability to distinguish main ideas from supporting details and to extract salient points to re-write them in the form of a summary. Candidates will be given clear indications of what they are to summarise and of the length of the summary.

Question 5 : There will be a number of short answer questions to test the candidates' knowledge of functional grammar, structure and usage.
All the items in this question will be compulsory. They will consist of correct use of prepositions, conjunctions, verbs and structure of sentences.

No specific book is being recommended for background reading.

Preparation Assessment Zone

Welcome to the Preparation Assessment Zone !

In this section, you'll find **ICSE Specimen Question Paper** and **Board Examination Paper 2024** to help you assess your readiness. Attempt these papers to familiarise yourself with the exam format and identify areas that need improvement.

Progress Tracker **Tick the papers as you complete them.**

- ☐ ICSE Specimen Question Paper
- ☐ Board Examination Paper 2024

ICSE Specimen Paper 2025

Session 2024-25

English Language 10th (Code 01)

Class 10

General Instructions

1. You will not be allowed to write during the first 15 minutes.
2. This time is to be spent in reading the question paper.
3. The time given at the head of this Paper is the time allowed for writing the answers.
4. Attempt all five questions.
5. The intended marks for questions or parts of questions are given in brackets [].
6. You are advised to spend not more than 30 minutes in answering Question 1 and 20 minutes in answering Question 2.

- No. of Questions : 5
- Time Alloted : 2 Hrs.
- Max. Marks : 80

Question 1.

(Do not spend more than 30 minutes on this question.)

Write a composition (300-350 words) on any one of the following **(20)**

(i) Write an original short story in which a woman, her strange neighbour and a police officer form the main characters.

(ii) Your teacher has asked you to form a group and work on a particular project. Write an account of how you worked together and what each of you learned from the experience.

(iii) *'Peer pressure is a force for good.'*

Express your views either for or against this statement.

(iv) Describe the locality in which you live. Give details of the things you see and hear as you walk around your locality. What do you especially like about the place?

(v) Study the picture given below. Write a story or a description on an account of what it suggests to you. Your composition may be about the subject of the picture or you may take suggestions from it; however, there must be a clear connection between the picture and your composition.

Question 2.

(Do not spend more than 20 minutes on this question.) **[10]**

Select any one of the following

(i) Your uncle was unable to attend your birthday celebration but has sent you one thousand rupees as a gift. Write a letter thanking him, tell him how you will spend the money and why you have made that particular choice.

(ii) The garbage bins in your locality have not been cleared regularly resulting in the overflow of garbage in the area. Write a letter to the Municipal Commissioner of your city/town complaining about the problem. Offer suggestions for the removal of the garbage and cleaning up of the place.

Question 3.

(i) Your school is hosting an Art and Craft exhibition. Write a notice informing the pupils at your school about the event. **[5]**

(ii) Write an e-mail to a local artist inviting him/her to inaugurate the exhibition and be the Chief Guest on the occasion. **[5]**

Question 4.

Read the following passage carefully and answer the questions that follow

One day, I found the pond occupied by several buffaloes. Their keeper, a boy a little older than me, was swimming about in the middle. Instead of climbing out on the bank, he would pull himself up on the back of one of his buffaloes, stretch his naked brown body out on the animal's glistening ***hide***, and start singing to himself.

When he saw me staring at him from across the pond, he smiled, showing gleaming white teeth on a dark face. He invited me to join him in a swim. I told him I couldn't swim, and he offered to teach me.

His name was Ramu, and he promised to give me swimming lessons every afternoon, and so it was during the afternoons - especially summer afternoons when everyone was asleep-that we usually met. Before long, I was able to swim across the pond to sit with Ramu astride a ***contented*** buffalo.

Sometimes, I would slip into the water. Emerging in shades of green and khaki, I would sneak into the house through the bathroom and bathe under the tap before getting into my clothes.

One afternoon, Ramu and I found a small tortoise in the mud sitting over a hole in which it had laid several eggs. I presented the tortoise to Grandfather. He had a weakness for tortoises, and was pleased with this addition to his menagerie, giving it a large tub of water all to itself, with an island of rocks in the middle. If one of the dogs bothered it too much, it would draw its head and legs into its shell and defy all its attempts at rough play.

Ramu came from a family of bonded labourers and had received no schooling. But he was well-versed in folklore and knew a great deal about birds and animals.

'Many birds are sacred,' said Ramu, as we watched a blue jay swoop down from a peepul tree and carry off a grasshopper.

Both Ramu and Grandfather were of the opinion that we should be more gentle with birds and animals and should not kill so many of them.

'It is also important that we respect them, said Grandfather. 'We must acknowledge their rights. Birds and animals are finding it more difficult to survive, because we are trying to destroy both them and their forests.'

Ramu and I spent long summer afternoons at the pond. I still remember him with affection, though we never saw each other again after I left Dehra.

—*Rusty, the Boy from the Hills, Ruskin Bond*

(i) For each word given below, choose the correct meaning (as used in the passage) from the options provided [2]

1. hide (line 3)
   (a) blanket (b) fur (c) undisclosed (d) skin

2. contented (line 10)
   (a) cheerful (b) lazy
   (c) satisfied (d) container

(ii) Which word in the passage is the opposite of 'easy'? [1]
   (a) sneak (b) difficult (c) labourer (d) survive

(iii) Answer the following questions briefly in your own words.
   (a) What did Ramu like to do once he had climbed on the back of a buffalo? [2]
   (b) What offer did Ramu make to the narrator? [2]
   (c) Why do you think the narrator would bathe before entering the house? [2]
   (d) Who was the large tub of water for? [1]
   (e) How would the tortoise protect itself from the dogs? [2]

(iv) Despite the lack of schooling, what did Ramu know? How, according to Ramu and Grandfather, should we treat birds and animals? Answer in not more than fifty words. [8]

Question 5.

(i) Fill in each of the numbered blanks with the correct form of the word given in brackets. Do not copy the passage but write in correct serial order the word or phrase appropriate to the blank space. [4]

Example:

(0) The Sun .... (shine) bright outside.

Answer: shone

It was hot in the railway compartment and the fan .... (1) (not work).

The elderly lady .... (2) (use) up all her water because she had cheerfully shared it with her fellow passengers. She knew that the train .... (3) (halt) at the station for only three minutes. Calling a shoeshine boy, she said, 'Will you help me? I .... (4) (need) a bottle of cold water and here is the money,' and she put a twenty rupee note in his hand. The boy snatched the money and .... (5) (disappear) into the crowd on the platform. A fellow passenger .... (6) (cannot believe) what he had witnessed. 'What .... (7) (you do)?" He said, 'You .... (8) (never see) your money again. Just then, the whistle was heard and the train began to move. At that moment, the child appeared at the window with the water. 'Your water,' he gasped, out of breath. 'And the change.'

(ii) Fill in the blanks with appropriate words. [4]

(a) We can cut ...... this field instead of taking the main road.
(b) Passengers are advised ...... standing on the footboard of a moving bus.
(c) They have been working on the project ...... years now.
(d) Ever ...... the accident, he has been afraid of boarding buses.
(e) It is a hard climb ...... the hill.
(f) She turned ...... the offer because she did not like the terms and conditions.
(g) I will need to speak ...... my parents before I sign up for the school trip.
(h) The sports teacher was taken ...... when he heard how enthusiastic the team was.

(iii) Join the following sentences to make one complete sentence **without using *and, but*** or ***so***. Choose the correct option. [4]

1. Stay still. We cannot take your photograph otherwise.
   (a) Stay still, else we cannot take your photograph otherwise.
   (b) Stay still because we can take your photograph otherwise.
   (c) Unless you stay still, we cannot take your photograph.
   (d) If you stay still, we cannot take your photograph.
2. Roy's mother rang up the school office. She wanted to enquire about the swimming classes at the summer camp.
   (a) Roy's mother rang up the school office as she want to enquire about the swimming classes at the summer camp.
   (b) Roy's mother rang up the school office to enquire about the swimming classes at the summer camp.
   (c) Roy's mother has rung up the school office to enquire about the swimming classes at the summer camp.
   (d) Roy's mother rang up the school office wanting enquiry about the swimming classes at the summer camp.
3. I left my keys somewhere. Do you know where they are?
   (a) Do you know where I had left my keys?
   (b) Do you know where my keys were left behind?
   (c) Do you know where I left my keys?
   (d) Do you know where I would have left my keys?
4. The captain should not be blamed for the team's defeat. The players should not be blamed for the team's defeat.
   (a) The captain should neither be blamed nor the players should be blamed for the team's defeat.
   (b) Neither the captain nor the players should be blamed for the team's defeat.
   (c) The captain should not be blamed for the team's defeat as the players should not be blamed for the team's defeat.
   (d) The captain should not be blamed for the team's defeat but the players too should not be blamed for the team's defeat.

(iv) Choose the correct option to rewrite the following according to the instructions given after each sentence. [8]

1. The audience broke into loud applause as soon as he finished speaking. *(Begin with: No sooner...)*
   (a) No sooner he finished speaking that the audience broke into loud applause.
   (b) No sooner had he finish speaking when the audience broke into loud applause.
   (c) No sooner did he finish speaking than the audience broke into loud applause.
   (d) No sooner the audience broke into loud applause than he finished speaking.
2. The news surprised everyone in my family. *(Begin with: The news took ...)*
   (a) The news took everyone in my family by surprise.
   (b) The news took everyone in my family with surprise.
   (c) The news took with surprise everyone in my family.
   (d) The news took everyone in my family for a surprise.
3. Yesterday was so much fun. *(End with a question tag)*
   (a) Yesterday was so much fun, would you say?
   (b) Was yesterday much fun?
   (c) Yesterday was so much fun, isn't it?
   (d) Yesterday was so much fun, wasn't it?
4. I wouldn't eat that food if I was not really hungry. *(Use: 'unless')*
   (a) Unless I eat that food I will remain really hungry.
   (b) I wouldn't be really hungry unless I ate that food.
   (c) I wouldn't eat that food unless I was not really hungry.
   (d) I wouldn't eat that food unless I was really hungry.
5. It is so hot and humid that I cannot sleep. *(Use: too)*
   (a) It is hot and humid too sleep.
   (b) It is too hot and humid to sleep.
   (c) It is hot and humid too so I cannot sleep.
   (d) It is too hot and humid such that I cannot sleep.
6. I prefer going out with friends to staying alone at home. *(Begin with: I would rather...)*
   (a) I would rather go out with friends than stay alone at home.
   (b) I would rather prefer going out with friends than staying alone at home.
   (c) I would rather prefer to go out with friends than stay alone at home.
   (d) I would rather go out with friends to staying alone at home.
7. "Why were you absent yesterday?", the teacher asked me. *(Begin with: The teacher asked me why...)*
   (a) The teacher asked me why was I absent yesterday.
   (b) The teacher asked me why I had been absent yesterday.
   (c) The teacher asked me why I had been absent the day before.
   (d) The teacher asked me why was I absent the day before.
8. Very few dancers are as graceful as she is. *(Begin with: She is...)*
   (a) She is one of the most graceful dancers.
   (b) She is the most graceful dancer.
   (c) She is more graceful than all the other dancers.
   (d) She is more graceful than a few other dancers.

Answers in Topper's Style

1. (i) In the small town of Willow Creek, Chaahat lived a solitary life after losing her family to flash floods. She had been living in the town for four years and had heard stories about many supernatural things happening in town. She never believed in them but, when she used to hear about them, she would get sacred. She believed that supernatural things were related to her neighbour, Mr. Henderson whom she always found to be a bit peculiar. The old man rarely left his house and, when he did, it was usually to tend to his chaotic garden and his hideous garden gnomes. Chaahat often watched him from her window, curious about his solitary life and his garden.

One chilly autumn evening, Chaahat found a small, intricately carved box on her doorstep. Assuming it was a misdelivered parcel, she decided to give it back to the post office the next morning. When she reached the post office, she was shocked that the address was hers. She did not have any idea what it was and whom it was from. So, she went to her neighbour suspecting it belonged to him. However, the moment Mr. Henderson saw the box, his face turned pale and he vehemently denied it was his. Perplexed but intrigued, Chaahat took the box home and set it on her mantelpiece.

Days passed and local rumours about a series of small thefts in the neighbourhood began to circulate. Items were mysteriously disappearing from homes, only to be found elsewhere in the town. The local police, led by Officer Arjun, were baffled having no leads or suspects.

One afternoon, Officer Arjun knocked on Chaahat's door inquiring if she had noticed any unusual activities around her home. Chaahat mentioned the strange box and her interaction with Mr. Henderson. Curious, Officer Arjun asked to examine the box. Upon inspection, he discovered a false bottom, revealing several stolen items including a vintage watch and a couple of old coins which had earlier been reported missing. Later, Officer Arjun and Chaahat visited Mr. Henderson with the box. Faced with the evidence, Mr. Henderson confessed but not to theft. He admitted that he had been finding these items in his garden, unearthed by his gnomes which seemed to move and rob people at night. Ashamed, he had tried to rid himself of the gnomes but they always seemed to come back.

Amused yet sympathetic, Officer Arjun decided to keep the matter quiet attributing the recovered items to their rightful owners. Chaahat, now viewing her neighbour with new understanding and a touch of fondness, offered to help him find what is happening with his gnomes. In this odd trio, a friendship blossomed, rooted in the peculiar mysteries of Willow Creek.

(ii) Working on a group project can be a rewarding experience, filled with challenges and opportunities for learning all the while strengthening your bonds with your friends and team mates. Recently, our teacher assigned a team-based project to our class on the various economics related topics that we have studied in our syllabi. The first task was to form teams which our teacher had already done. Then, we had to select our topic. Fortunately, my team had some of my childhood friends and after a lot of discussion we decided to take up migration as a topic. To complete the project, we had to submit a report and also make a presentation on our chosen topic.

For the project, my team decided to talk to different daily wage labourers that we can find around us. I took on the responsibility for the presentation part focusing on designing slides and preparing the speech. Other members, Jay and Mohak, conducted deep research compiling data and case studies while Mayank and Richa worked on writing the content and ensuring it flowed logically. Doing the project was easy as we were organised. Moreover, it not only enhanced our understanding of the Subject but also taught us valuable lessons in teamwork and individual responsibility.

Throughout the project, communication was our biggest asset. We set up weekly meetings to discuss our progress and address any issues. These meetings helped us stay aligned with our goals and maintain a cohesive approach. Through these interactions, I learned the importance of clear and consistent communication in keeping a team on track.

Each team member brought a unique perspective to the project which enriched our final output. For example, Jay and Mohak's detailed research introduced us to different reasons for migration starting from better livelihood to religious intolerance. Richa's writing skills helped articulate complex ideas in a way that was easy to understand and Mayank's keen eye for details ensured that our content was accurate and thorough.

Presenting our project to the class was a highlight. It was a moment of pride for all of us seeing our collective efforts come together seamlessly. The positive feedback from our teacher and peers was gratifying and reaffirmed the value of our hard work.

From this group project, I learned that successful collaboration requires patience, respect for others' ideas and an openness to learn from one another. Each member taught me something different whether it was a new fact about environmental conservation or a better way to communicate ideas. This project was not just about the environmental topics we explored but also about discovering each other's strengths and capabilities, making it a truly enriching experience.

(iii) **For the Motion**

The pressure to conform to do what others are doing can be powerful and hard to resist. A person might feel pressured to do something just because others are doing it. The pressure becomes even more powerful when it comes from one's peers or friends. Peer pressure is a phenomenon that can influence a person to do something because one's peers are doing it.

Peer pressure is often painted in a negative light evoking images of young individuals being coerced into harmful behaviours or adopting unhealthy habits. However, when channelled positively, peer pressure can be a powerful force for good. It can encourage individuals to strive for a better performance and adopt healthier lifestyles, thereby fostering personal growth and development.

One of the most significant benefits of positive peer pressure is its ability to motivate individuals towards excellence. In educational settings, the influence of peers who prioritise their studies can be contagious. For instance, students who see their friends dedicating time to homework and preparing diligently for exams are likely to feel motivated to mirror these productive behaviours. This form of peer pressure can create a supportive environment where students push each other to achieve their best, ultimately raising the academic standards of the entire group.

Moreover, peer pressure can promote healthy social behaviours and ethical standards. Young people learn a great deal about social interactions from their peers. When surrounded by friends who respect others, engage in community service and uphold integrity, individuals adopt these positive traits. This leads to a more compassionate and responsible community.

Additionally, peer pressure can be a pivotal force in discouraging negative habits. For example, a group of friends can influence a member to stop smoking or reduce alcohol consumption. The desire to fit in and be accepted can motivate individuals to make healthier lifestyle choices which might be difficult to undertake alone.

However, the positive outcomes of peer pressure depend significantly on the group dynamics and the prevailing attitudes within a peer group. It is crucial for individuals, especially young people, to choose their friends wisely. Being part of a group that values positive and constructive behaviours can transform peer pressure into a beneficial force that enhances one's life.

In conclusion, peer pressure undoubtedly has the potential to be a force for good. It encourages excellence, promotes ethical behaviour and supports healthy lifestyle choices. Like any tool, the impact of peer pressure depends on how it is used. If leveraged positively, it can lead to personal and communal improvement.

Against the Motion

We all share the need to connect with others, no matter our age. We want a sense of belonging at home and within the community. Being accepted by peers is an important part of adolescence. Teens yearn to fit in and to be seen in a favourable light. As a result, peers often have a strong influence on teen behaviours, choices and actions. More often than not, peer pressure takes a negative turn. Hence, I do not agree with the statement— 'Peer pressure is a force for good'.

The impact and scope of influence of peer pressure is so adverse that it has a negative impact on an individual. Friends or peers may encourage engaging in risky things such as doing drugs, reckless driving, alcoholic habit, bunking classes, etc. As a result, one could get distracted and go on a path that ruins one's future.

The impact of peers can be easily found in the age of social media wherein individuals participate in reckless acts to fit in with peers. They try to follow the standard and, in doing so, go against their values and belief systems. Often, children, enticed with what their friends have, become entitled and show immature behaviour. They even participate in illegal activities to fulfill their need to fit in.

If an individual does not fit in and give in to peer pressure, he/she is often bullied to the point that the person develops mental health problems and even causes self-harm. Now and then, the effect of peer tension on young teenagers is disrupting to the point that they can barely remain in their skin, are separated from loved ones and become discouraged and restless.

Thus, peer pressure is not a force for good.

(iv) Locality refers to the specific geographical area or neighbourhood in which a community of people live and work. It is a fundamental concept that helps define the character, culture and identity of a particular place. The term is often used to describe the unique features of a specific region as well as the social connections and shared experiences of its residents.

One of the most important aspects of locality is the sense of community that it fosters. Whether it is a small town, a large city neighbourhood or a rural area, a locality can create a strong sense of belonging and shared identity among its residents. This sense of community is often built around common interests, traditions and values which are strengthened by the interactions and relationships between people in the area.

I live in a great residential locality in Delhi. It is society with multiple complexes. There is a huge park nearby with lush greenery and many different kinds of birds. Multiple amenities are easily accessible in my locality. We have three malls which are 10 minutes ride away with many big brands and eateries. There are also many famous street food stalls which offer a diverse range of food options. From vegetarian delights to international cuisines, you'll find it all here. The nearby market is bustling with a variety of snacks, chaat, candies and cuisines. And, the best part? You can enjoy all this in one place from hotdogs and momos to hot and cold beverages like coffees, teas, milkshakes and juices.

Another gem is the local market. From 10:30 a.m. until 8:30 p.m., it's a bustling market with hundreds of retailers selling anything and everything. But, as evening descends, this place undergoes a magical transformation into a foodie's paradise. The aroma of Gulab jamun, Dahi vada, Samosa, Dosa, Pav bhaji, Pani puri, Chinese food and Soft beverages fills the air. You'll also find mobile food vendors here. This market focuses on traditional Indori food. Poha Jalebi merits special mention, as it is the city's king of street food. Poha is available at all times, 24 hours a day, 365 days a year.

Overall, it is a fantastic and well-known street market in my city where people enjoy shopping.

(v) He was the funniest boy I had ever met. He would make everyone laugh even in the most trying times. Blessed with a funny nature, Varun would make everyone forget his/her worries in his company. No amount of sadness could dampen his spirit.

I remember once three of us friends including Roshni and Varun and I had failed the chemistry exam badly. Our parents had been called and we were told that we would have to repeat a year. That was a very hard time but, even then, no look of worry could be spotted on Varun's face or in his behaviour. His cheer remained undiminished even when his father suffered a major financial loss in business. Even during that time, Varun was known to spread cheer around. He always pushed his worries to the backseat and dedicated himself towards making others happy.

However, the loss of Varun's pet Munch, a few months ago, immersed him in grief. That was the only time that robbed him of his smiling face. For days, he did not speak to anyone and shut himself up in his room. We could not see him like that so Roshni and I decided to do something to dispel his gloom.

One day, we all went to his place and rang the doorbell of his house. There, we kept a little box, slightly open from one side and hid ourselves so that he could not see us. When he opened the door, he was surprised to find no one. He picked up the box with a look of amazement on his face. He took the lid off and out came a puppy, quite like Munch. He held it in his hands and started to play with it. It brought his smile back. Then, we all came into the sight and shouted with excitement, 'Surprise!'

Indeed, that little effort from our end helped Varun come out of his sorrow. Later, we played with the puppy and, then, went to the park. We played till late in the evening and enjoyed as our friend was back again.

2. (i) XYZ Apartments
PQR City

14th July, 20XX

Dear Uncle,

I hope this letter finds you in the best of health and spirits. I am well and happy here. I have written to tell you that it upset me that you couldn't attend my birthday party. At the same time, I want to thank you for the money (1000 rupees) that you sent me as a birthday gift. I can't tell you how much I appreciate it. It really means a lot to me that you remembered my special day. I've already put your gift to good use. I have given it as fee for an educational tour that our school is organising to Amritsar. We will be going to the Wagah border, the Jallianwallah Bagh, the Golden temple and many other places.

I am grateful for your generosity and support. You've always been an amazing uncle to me and I feel truly blessed to have you in my life.

Thank you again for your kindness and thoughtfulness. I hope we can catch up soon and celebrate properly.

Yours loving,

XYZ

(ii) 202, M.G. Road,
Agra

27th July, 20XX

The Municipal Commissioner,
Municipal Corporation,
Agra

Subject Complaint regarding overflowing garbage and lack of cleanliness in locality

Dear Sir/Ma'am,

Through this letter, I would like to draw your attention to the overflowing garbage and lack of cleanliness in M.G. Road, Agra. It is a matter of great disappointment that in the times when the entire country is striving towards cleanliness and sanitation, our locality presents a picture of dirt. It is not the lack of garbage bins or cleaning staff, but the lack of action on the part of the staff that the bins are always overflowing. As a result, there is a bad odour in the locality and people are becoming prone to diseases.

Hence, I request you to solve this problem and ensure that the locality maintains its cleanliness. For the same, I suggest that garbage vans and staff should come regularly to clean the locality. Further, regular inspection can ensure that the system is effective in its implementation. With your aid, we would be able to move ahead in our path towards cleanliness.

Thanking you,

Yours faithfully,

ABC

3. (i) **Mix and Mould**

Inter School Art and Craft Competition

Date : Friday, 3rd August, 20XX

Time : 10.00 am—3.00 pm

Venue : The Assembly Area, ABC School

All the interested students should submit their names to their respective Class Teachers by 20th July, 20XX.

(ii) **E-mail-id** xyz@gmail.com

Subject Invite to inaugurate the Arts and Crafts exhibition as a Chief Guest

Respected Sir/Ma'am,
With great pleasure and pride, ABC School would like to inform in that it is organising an Arts and Crafts Exhibition on 3rd August, Friday from 10.00 a.m. to 3.00 p.m. in the Assembly Area, ABC School. For the same, we would be honoured if you could inaugurate and grace the exhibition as the Chief Guest.

With your valuable experience and knowledge, students would be motivated to participate in creative activities and take up art as a proper career. Hoping for a positive reply.

Anticipating a positive response,

Yours faithfully,
PQR

4. (i) 1. (d) skin

2. (c) satisfied

(ii) (b) difficult

(iii) (a) Once he had climbed the back of the buffalo, Ramu liked to stretch his naked brown body out on the animal's glistening hide/back and start singing to himself.

(b) Ramu offered to teach the narrator to swim every afternoon.

(c) The narrator would bathe before entering the house to avoid being scolded for swimming in the village pond when everyone was asleep. He thought that his elders become angry so he would sneak into the house through the bathroom and bathe under the tap to get clean first.

(d) The large tub of water was for the tortoise presented by the narrator to his grandfather.

(e) To protect itself from the dogs, the tortoise would draw its head and legs into its shell and defy all the dogs' attempts at rough play.

(iv) Despite the lack of schooling, Ramu was well-versed in folklore and knew a great deal about birds and animals. He also knew that many birds were sacred and that we should not kill so many of them. According to Ramu and his grandfather, we should be gentler with birds and animals. We should respect and acknowledge their rights and not destroy their forests.

5. (i) 1. was not working
2. had used
3. halted/would halt
4. need
5. disappeared
6. could not believe
7. are you doing
8. will never see

(ii) a. across
b. against
c. for
d. since
e. up
f. down
g. to
h. aback

(iii) 1. (c) Unless you stay still, we cannot take your photograph.
2. (b) Roy's mother rang up the school office to enquire about the swimming classes at the summer camp.
3. (c) Do you know where I left my keys?
4. (b) Neither the captain nor the players should be blamed for the team's defeat.

(iv) 1. (c) No sooner did he finish speaking than the audience broke into loud applause.
2. (a) The news took everyone in my family by surprise.
3. (d) Yesterday was so much fun, wasn't it?
4. (d) I wouldn't eat that food unless I was really hungry.
5. (b) It is too hot and humid to sleep.
6. (a) I would rather go out with friends than stay alone at home.
7. (c) The teacher asked me why I had been absent the day before.
8. (a) She is one of the most graceful dancers.

ICSE Solved Paper 2024

English Language Paper-1 (Code 01)

Class 10

General Instructions

1. You will not be allowed to write during the first 15 minutes. This time is to be spent in reading the question paper.
2. The time given at the head of this paper is the time allowed for writing the answers.
3. Attempt all five questions.
4. The intended marks for questions or parts of questions are given in brackets [ ].
5. You are advised to spend not more than 30 minutes in answering Question 1 and 20 minutes in answering Question 2.

- No. of Questions : 5
- Time Alloted : 2 Hrs.
- Max. Marks : 80

Question 1

(Do not spend more than 30 minutes on this question.)

1. Write a composition (300 - 350) words on **any one** of the following. **[20]**

(i) Write an original short story entitled 'A Strange Visitor'.

(ii) Narrate an incident from your experience in which your parents had entrusted you with a difficult task. Give details of the task, how you carried it out and your feelings at the end.

(iii) Describe how you spend your time on a holiday afternoon. Why do you think it is necessary to have these times of quietness and solitude ?

(iv) Express your views either for or against the statement ' Junk food should be banned'.

(v) Study the picture given below. Write a story or a description or an account of what it suggest to you. Your composition may be about the subject of the picture or you may take suggestions form it; however, there must be a clear connection between the picture and your composition.

Question 2

(Do not spend more than 20 minutes on this question.)

2. Select **any one** of the following. **[10]**

(i) Your friend was absent from school on a day when an unfortunate incident took place for which you were blamed. Write a letter to your friend giving details about the incident, your role in it and how the matter was finally resolved.

(ii) You wish to stage a play to create awareness about the importance of saving electricity. Write a letter to the Manager of a nearby shopping mall / supermarket requesting permission to use the space in front of the shopping mall/supermarket to stage the play. Give him / her details about your requirements and state why the play will be beneficial to the shoppers.

Question 3

3. (i) Your school is hosting an Inter-School Dance Competition. Write a notice to be put up on your school notice board informing the students about the event. **[5]**

(ii) Write an e-mail to the Principal of a neighbouring school to request him / her to send their dance teacher to act as a judge for the competition. **[5]**

Question 4

4. Read the following passage carefully and answer the questions that follow.

Ashamanja Babu lived in a small flat in Bhowanipore. A Clerk in the registry department of Lajpat Rai Post office, Ashamanja Babu was fortunate as he could walk to his office in seven minutes flat without having to fight his way into the buses and trains of Calcutta. He lived a rather carefree life as he was not the kind of person to sit and brood about what might have been had Fate been kinder to him. On the whole, he was quite content with his lot. Two Hindi films and fish twice a week-these were enough to keep him happy. The only thing that **perturbed** him at times was his lack of companionship. A bachelor with few friends and relatives, he often wished he had a dog to keep him company. It need not be a huge Alsation like the one owned by the Talukdars, who lived two houses down the lane; it could be any ordinary little dog which would follow him around morning and evening, wag its tail when he came home from work and obey his orders faithfully.

Ashamanja Babu's secret desires were that he would speak to his dog in English, ' Stand up ', ' Sit down', ' Shake hands' - How nice it would be if his dog obeyed such commands! That would make him really happy.

On a cloudy day marked by a steady drizzle, Ashamanja Babu went to the market in Hashimara to buy some oranges. At one end of the market, beside a **stunted** Kul tree, sat a man. As their eyes met, the man smiled. Was he a beggar? His clothes made him look like one. Ashamanja Babu noticed at least five sewning-on patches on his trousers and jacket. But the man didn't have a begging bowl. Instead, by his side was a shoe - box with a little pup sticking its head out of it.

'Good morning !' said the man in English. Ashamanja Babu was obliged to return the greeting. 'Buy dog? Dog buy? Very good dog.' The man had taken the pup out of the box and had put it down on the ground. 'Very cheap. Very good. Happy dog?'

The pup shook the raindrops off its coat, looked at Ashamanja Babu and wagged its minuscule two inch tail. Ashamanja Babu moved closer to the pup.

Crouched on the ground and stretched out his hand. The pup gave his ring finger a lick with its pink tongue. Nice, Friendly dog.

'How much? What price?'

'Ten rupees'

A little haggling and the price came down to seven rupees. Ashamanja Babu paid the money, put the pup back in the shoe box, closed the lid to save it form the drizzle, and turned homewards, forgetting all about the oranges. *–Ashamanja Babu's Dog by Satyajit Ray* [30]

(i) For each word given below, choose the correct meaning (as used in the passage) from the options provided. [2]

1. perturbed *(line 6)*
   (a) frightened (b) unsettled
   (c) confused (d) mocked

2. stunted (line 15)
   (a) prevented from growing (b) prepared for tricks
   (c) prevented from taking action (d) allowed to do stunts

(ii) Which word in the passage means the opposite of the word 'expensive' ? [1]
   (a) carefree (b) ordinary
   (c) cheap (d) haggling

(iii) Answer the following questions briefly in your own words.
   (a) What kept Ashamanja Babu happy? [2]
   (b) What does this tell you about him? [2]
   (c) What is that one other thing he needed to complete his happiness? [1]
   (d) Why did Ashamanja Babu think the man was a beggar? [2]
   (e) Why did Ashamanja Babu forget about his oranges? [2]

(iv) In not more than 50 words, narrate the series of events from the time the puppy was taken out of the box till it was paid for. [8]

Question 5

5. (i) Fill in each of the numbered blanks with the correct form of the word given in brackets. Do not copy the passage but write in correct serial order the word or phrase appropriate to the blank space. [4]

Example

Next day, my uncle (0) .... (spend) a lot of time.

Answer: (0) Spent

He (1) .... (select) clothes for me, and my aunt (2) .... (give) my face a scrub and (3) .... (groom) me. My uncle (4) .... (follow) me about (5) .... (utter) several pieces of advice before (6) .... (let) me out, 'You must never scowl even if the Sun (7) .... (hit) you in the eyes. You must try (8) .... (look) pleasant.'

(ii) Fill in the blanks with appropriate words. [4]
   (a) There's a black cat sitting .... the wall.
   (b) The horse jumped .... the hedge.
   (c) Mother goes .... the market every day.
   (d) Several people have climbed Mount Everest .... recent years.
   (e) I often go to school .... my friend.
   (f) I have left my keys .... home.
   (g) Instead of talking, prove your worth .... doing something.
   (h) I have not slept .... yesterday.

(iii) Choose the correct option to make one complete sentence **without using and, but or so.** [4]

1. The magician took pity on the mouse. He turned it into a cat.
   (a) Showing pity on the mouse, he turned it into a cat.
   (b) Taking pity on the mouse, he turned it into a cat.

(c) The magician turned the mouse into a cat by taking pity .
(d) Taking pity on the mouse, the magician turned it into a cat.

2. This work must be completed. There is a deadline.
(a) Since this work must be completed, there is a deadline.
(b) This work must be completed because there is a deadline.
(c) This work must be completed though there is a deadline.
(d) This work must be completed when there is a deadline.

3. He fled somewhere. His pursuers could not follow him.
(a) He fled where his pursuers could not follow him.
(b) He pursued somewhere his followers could be flee.
(c) He fled somewhere when his pursuers could not follow him.
(d) He fled where his pursuers cannot follow him.

4. He began late. He finished first.
(a) He finished first and began late
(b) He began first but finished late.
(c) Though he finished late, he began first.
(d) Though he began late, he finished first.

(iv) Choose the correct option and rewrite the sentence according to the instruction given after each. [8]

1. Arun and Nikhil had climbed the mountain.
(Add a question tag)
(a) Arun and Nikhil had climbed the mountain, didn't they?
(b) Arun and Nikhil had climbed the mountain, had they?
(c) Arun and Nikhil had climbed the mountain, hadn't they?
(d) Arun and Nikhil had climbed the mountain, did they?

2. The children have broken the window pane.
(Begin The window pane ....)
(a) The window pane had been broken by the children.
(b) The window pane has been broken by the children.
(c) The window pane has not been broken by the children.
(d) The window pane had not been broken by the children.

3. The apples are so cheap that they cannot be good.
(Use : 'too')
(a) The apples are too cheap and good.
(b) The apples are to cheap as well as good.
(c) The apples are too good to be cheap.
(d) The apples are too cheap to be good.

4. She is very clever and beautiful.
(Use : 'not only')
(a) Not only is she very clever but also beautiful.
(b) Not only was she beautiful and she was also clever.
(c) Not only is she clever she was also very beautiful.
(d) Not only was she very beautiful but is also clever.

5. I prefer a simple vanilla ice cream to fancy desserts.
(Begin : I would rather ....)
(a) I would rather have a simple vanilla ice cream to fancy desserts.
(b) I would rather have a simple vanilla ice cream than fancy desserts.
(c) I would rather prefer a simple vanilla ice cream than fancy desserts.
(d) I would rather have a vanilla ice cream than a fancy dessert.

6. He asked, "When do you intend to make the payment?"
(Begin : He asked ....)
(a) He asked when he did intend to make the payment.
(b) He asked when she is intending to make the payment.
(c) He asked when I intended to make the payment.
(d) He asked when they are intending to make the payment.

7. If the rain does not stop, Mariam will not be able to do the laundry.
(Begin : Unless ....)
(a) Unless the rain does not stop, Mariam will not be able to do the laundry.
(b) Unless Mariam does the laundry, the rain will not stop.
(c) Unless the rain stop, Mariam will not be able to do the laundry.
(d) Unless the rain stops, Mariam will not be able to do the laundry.

8. This is the best movie I have ever seen.
(Begin : Never ....)
(a) Never had I seen a good movie than this.
(b) Never I have seen a better movie than this.
(c) Never have I seen a better movie than this.
(d) I have never seen a good movie as this.

Answers *in Topper's Style*

1. (i)

A Strange Visitor

It was a bleak and sad day for I was knee deep in debt and with no resource to pay for it. Unfortunately, I had unconsciously become a part of a fraud scheme and had given up all my savings in it. Due to my job, I had been unable to look into the scheme and was satisfied that I was getting huge returns. Consequently, I had lived a modest and fulfilling life. My happiness was snatched a few months back when the reality came out and I found that the organisers of the scheme had racked up many debts in my name. Further, only I had to pay for it as the scammers were nowhere to be found.

Much like other days, that day too, my mind was filled with these thoughts and my mistakes. With sadness, anger and many other emotions, I went outside to look around. It was a cold frosty morning. The fields were white and scenic but cold. I lived in rural Ireland which was very quiet. By the side of my house, there is a large stone and that's nothing unusual as Ireland is full of large stones. Some stones are said to be Fairy Stones which is believed to take living form to help those in need.

However, that day someone was sitting on one stone. As I went near the person, I saw that it was a very charismatic looking man. I did not recognise him. Moreover, his funny clothes made it seem like he was not of the time. He looked to be freezing so I asked him if he was ok but he didn't reply. I asked him if he was hungry, no response again. I asked him into the house to warm himself. I went in before him and left the door open behind me.

After a few moments he came in, stood at the door, looked around and sat on the stool near the open fire. I made him a cup of hot tea and offered him some baked bread and a few biscuits. He sat there and seemed to enjoy his tea but he did not speak a word to me.

After he had finished his tea, I took his cup from him and asked if there was anything else he would like. Just as he smiled, there was a knock at the front door. I opened it but there was no one there so I turned around to try to get the man to speak again. However, he was gone. I was baffled. Where had he gone? There was only one way out, which was by the front door. As I was wondering, I saw a pouch on the stool. Much to my surprise, it contained 20 gold coins. I think the man forgot it so I kept the coins for him. My situation has improved since then but the man did not come back.

(ii) I remember one incident where my parents gave me a difficult task to do which I was nervous about. It was about driving a car. I had been taking driving lessons for a few weeks by then and was fairly good at it. I used to go for my lessons thrice a week and was getting a hang of it. During one of those lessons, my father accompanied me and sat at the backseat while I was practising my skills. I felt somewhat nervous and intimidated but ended up doing quite well and my father even gave me a reassuring smile when we headed back home after the lesson.

The next day was Sunday and my parents had decided to go for a small outing to the City Mall for some lunch and shopping. I was excited and started getting dressed up for the outing. After I was dressed, I went downstairs to the living room to take out the keys to lock the house. As I was looking for the house keys in the drawer, my father asked me to bring the car keys as well. I took both the keys and gave the car keys to him. To my surprise, my father told me that he didn't need the car keys as it would be me who would be driving. I felt a little anxious as it would be my first time driving my parents in a car. But I took the keys from him and said that I would love to drive, without giving any hint that I was nervous. We left the house and I started driving slowly but attentively. I gained a fair speed after a few minutes and got a little confident. The rest of the drive went smoothly and we reached the mall in 15 minutes. I felt relieved that I did well without facing any obstacles. My parents gave me a proud and reassuring smile as they got out of the car and patted my back for the drive.

(iii) In this highly busy and competitive world, no one has free time. Usually, I do not have much time to relax either. However, when I do get a chance I do tend to utilise it to take a breather and spent some time relaxing. The concept of relaxing on a holiday afternoon means different things for different people. For me, it means a variety of things depending upon my mood. Generally, these things range from painting to watching a movie.

There are days when I am inspired by the attractive doodles and paintings on pinterest. With much enthusiasm, one day, I decided to do the mandala art of Goddess Saraswati. For the same, I gathered my art supplies and sat to work. It was a tiring process which took me 3 whole afternoons to complete but that art piece now resides in my grandparents' house as a framed photo.

Some days, you would find me watching latest movies on my home projector. I would sit on my couch, arrange for my food and randomly pick a movie which is generally either a comedy or a horror.

Spending my time doing nothing but giving my mind a break is essential for me. And I think it should be a necessity for everyone. These times of quiet and solitude help us reenergise for the coming days. If we do not take a break and do what makes us happy, our lives can take us on the path of burn-out or a situation wherein we are physically and mentally exhausted. In such situations, we do not wish to do anything and suffer from many lifestyle diseases.

Thus, a break from the hustle and bustle of life is required by our mind and body. In this break, we need to do what we want to do without anyone ordering us around or nagging us. This is our moment of peace, relaxation and joy away from the stress of life. Giving yourself the gift of 'me time' is important for your well-being all year, especially if you're feeling particularly stressed out.

(iv) **For the Motion**

Wise people, including our parents, have often been quoted to say that health is wealth. I stand, thus, for the motion 'Junk food should be banned'. It is only the foolish who choose not to listen.

Junk food is an umbrella term that refers to highly processed and calorie-dense foods that are low in nutritional value. These foods often contain high levels of unhealthy ingredients such as sugar, salt, unhealthy fats and artificial additives. These food items affect the human body in a number of ways. The short term effects include energy spikes and crashes, bloating, constipation and dehydration. Various scientific studies and researches have associated junk food with many other lifelong illnesses including obesity, diabetes, heart disease, hypertension, tooth decay and cavities, and even nutritional deficiencies.

Eating junk food is similar to giving an open invitation to all the diseases in the world.

If you are a reasonable individual, then you will be aware of the fact that all living beings eat food to gain energy and to cultivate a strong body which can fight off diseases and ensure a painless existence. You will eat food to live a long, healthy life, one which is rid of medicines and supplements.

Unfortunately, youngsters cannot be trusted to make the right decisions for themselves. Hence, it is essential that the decision to stop partaking in this particular form of poison be taken for them. Considering the

significant risk to the health and wellbeing of humans as individuals and as a society, I support the complete ban of all non-nutritious junk food in a vision to create a healthier society.
Thank you.

Against the Motion

I agree with my opponent in the fact that junk food is often harmful to health and that it has practically nothing to say for its lack of nutritional value. I would also agree that it is in fact a slow poison! However, while it may not be nutritious and conducive to a healthy lifestyle, for many people, it is the only choice. The rushed lifestyle of the modern world does not allow people the time to carefully choose ingredients according to their nutritional value and cook it. Many people only have the time to cook two-minute noodles before rushing off to work. Would you stand in front of them and proclaim that just because they are not eating anything healthy, they cannot eat anything at all?

Junk food does serve a purpose after all. It may not be nutritious but it does fill the stomach. For the people with limited time and limited choices, junk food stands for comfort.

Moreover, in today's world, healthier food options are also more expensive and, thus, unaffordable to many. It is an ironic fact but one that the common people cannot do anything about. Although it is imperative that we cultivate good eating habits, unfortunately the ability to have a nutritious meal is not a necessity; it is a luxury. Organic and chemical-free food available in the market is much costlier than the junk food and difficult to access.

Therefore, the only way to ensure that people do not consume junk food, and to ban its production, is to produce organic and healthy food and make it available at affordable prices in the market. If more shops sell healthier alternatives at cheaper prices, the consumption of junk food will decrease eventually.

As of present, it is unwise to ban junk food as it would leave many people hungry. Thus, I stand against the motion 'Junk food should be banned'.

Thank you

(v) A few weeks back, I paid a visit to my Grandma's village which is located on the outskirts of a city. I was mesmerised by the straw and clay houses and the swings on the trees where children were playing and having fun. The whole atmosphere was very lively, energetic and surprisingly calm at the same time.
I felt relaxed to be away from the noisy city and being around nature.

After having some delicious lunch that my Grandma had prepared especially for me, I went out for a quick stroll around the village. The cool breeze under the shade of the trees felt really pleasant and comforting. As I was walking, I came across a bunch of small children sitting under a huge banyan tree. I walked towards them and saw that they were all sitting in a circle around a Carrom board which was placed on the ground near the tree's trunk. When the children saw me approaching, they looked at me and smiled. They asked me if I wanted to play to which I politely said no. I asked them about the Carrom board and to whom it belonged. The children rejoiced and said that they bought the Carrom board at the village fair with the money that my Grandma had given them. It was their first time playing with it. I felt such joy after hearing that my generous Grandma had given these kids money so that they could buy themselves this game to play together. The children then started to arrange all of the pucks together in a circle in the middle of the board. They also played rock, papers, scissors to decide who would play the first shot. Their excitement made me appreciate the little things in life, and taught me to enjoy every moment as it comes.

2. (i)

XYZ Apartments,
Delhi
8th February, 20XX

Dear Vayu,

I hope you are fine now. I missed you a lot during the exhausting day. I know you must be very curious to know why I called the day exhausting. Well, something happened and I was wrongly blamed for it. While going to the playground in a queue during recess, Ravi fell down the stairs which resulted in many serious injuries. When we all were asked about how it happened, Stuti blamed me saying that I was just behind him and must have pushed him as a revenge for the humiliating prank he did on me day before yesterday. I was shocked by such a blame. I agree I was angry but we had resolved the issue way before which many of our classmates pointed out.

Now, without further questioning, the school decided to call my parents. When they arrived, my parents were informed about the situation and my punishment- they were rusticating me. Can you believe it?

Calmly, my father reminded them of the CCTV cameras which had recently been installed. He asked to show him the footage so that he can see for himself if I really did this.

The school authorities were shocked that they had not thought of this. They hurriedly got the footage which clearly showed that I, in fact, was not immediately behind Ravi and that he had slipped on a banana peel. Looking at the truth, everyone was apologetic towards me. However, I was and still am hurt at the blame. The issue, though resolved, has shown me who my true friends are.

I just hope you were there today to see how bad it got. Get well soon so that we can visit Ravi.

Yours friendly,
PQR

(ii) 16, ABC Apartments,
Nashik

1st June, 20XX

The Manager,
XYZ Shopping Mall,
Nashik

Subject Staging a play to create Awareness

Dear Sir/Ma'am,

It is with great pleasure that I have written this letter to inform you on behalf of 'Live Happy Youth Club' that we are organising a small play to create awareness about the importance of saving electricity. For the same, I would request you to permit us to use the space in front of the shopping mall.

The play, though appears to be social, will increase footfall in your mall. While shopping is the main concern, event like ours will also include the entertainment aspect encouraging more and more people to visit the mall. Further, it will boost your overall sales.

I hope that you would consider our request and permit us to stage our play in your premises. Hoping for a positive response.

Thanking you,

Yours faithfully,
PQR
Secretary, Live Happy Youth Club

3. (i)

Dazzling Dancers
Inter-School Dance Competition
Date 31st January, 20XX
Time 11:00 am onwards
Venue Auditorium, XYZ School
Come, participate, cheer and witness the dancing extravaganza.

(ii) **To** principalpqr@gmail.com

Subject Invitation to judge the Inter-School Dance Competition

Dear Sir/Ma'am,

With great pleasure, I would like to inform you that XYZ School, Delhi is going to organise an Inter-School Dance Competition on 31st January, 20XX from 11:00 a.m. onwards in the school auditorium. For the same, we would love to have the dance teacher of your school over as a judge of the competition.

Kindly accept our invitation and increase the glory of the competition. Hoping for a positive response.

Thanking You,

Yours obediently,
ABC
Principal
XYZ School

4. (i) 1. (b) unsettled

2. (a) prevented from growing

(ii) (c) cheap

(iii) (a) Watching two Hindi films and having fish twice a week kept Ashamanja Babu happy.

(b) This tells us that he was a simple man who was content with his life.

(c) Since he was a bachelor, he longed for companionship to complete his happiness. He wished that he had a dog.

(d) Ashmanja Babu thought that the man was a beggar because his clothes had multiple patches sewn on them.

(e) Ashmanja Babu forgot about his oranges because he came across a puppy for sale which he eventually ended up buying.

(iv) The man took the pup out of the box and kept it on the ground. The pup looked at Ashmanja Babu and wagged his tiny tail. Ashmanja Babu bent down and stretched out his hand, and the dog licked his ring finger with its pink tongue. He then asked for the price when the man said "ten rupees". After some haggling, the price came down to seven rupees.

5. (i) 1. selected 2. gave 3. groomed 4. followed

5. uttering 6. letting 7. hits 8. to look

(ii) (a) on (b) over (c) to (d) in

(e) with (f) at (g) by (h) since

(iii) 1. (d) Taking pity on the mouse the magician turned it into a cat

2. (b) This work must be completed because there is a deadline.

3. (a) He fled where his pursuers could not follow him.

4. (d) Though he began late, he finished first.

(iv) 1. (c) Arun and Nikhil had climbed the mountain, hadn't they?

2. (b) The window pane has been broken by the children.

3. (d) The apples are too cheap to be good.

4. (a) Not only is she very clever but also beautiful.

5. (b) I would rather have a simple vanilla ice cream than fancy desserts.

6. (c) He asked when I intended to make the payment.

7. (d) Unless the rain stops, Mariam will not be able to do the laundry.

8. (c) Never have I seen a better movie than this.

II

Proficiency Building Zone

Welcome to the Proficiency Building Zone !

This section contains **10 Sample Question Papers** designed to enhance your problem-solving skills and proficiency. Use these papers to practice regularly and track your progress. Remember, consistent practice is key to mastering English Language.

Progress Tracker **Tick the papers as you complete them.**

- ☐ Sample Paper 1 ______ (Fill your score)
- ☐ Sample Paper 2 ______ (Fill your score)
- ☐ Sample Paper 3 ______ (Fill your score)
- ☐ Sample Paper 4 ______ (Fill your score)
- ☐ Sample Paper 5 ______ (Fill your score)
- ☐ Sample Paper 6 ______ (Fill your score)
- ☐ Sample Paper 7 ______ (Fill your score)
- ☐ Sample Paper 8 ______ (Fill your score)
- ☐ Sample Paper 9 ______ (Fill your score)
- ☐ Sample Paper 10 ______ (Fill your score)

SQP Code : **PB-1/10**

Series ***i*-Succeed 1-25/10**

Roll No. | | | | | | | | |

Sample Question Paper 01

English Language 10th (Code 01)

General Instructions

1. You will not be allowed to write during the first 15 minutes. This time is to be spent in reading the question paper.
2. The time given at the head of this paper is the time allowed for writing the answers.
3. Attempt all five questions.
4. The intended marks for questions or parts of questions are given in brackets [].
5. You are advised to spend not more than 30 minutes in answering Question 1 and 20 minutes in answering Question 2.

Time : 2 Hrs.

Max. Marks : 80

Question 1.

(Do not spend more than 30 minutes on this question)

Write a composition (300-350 words) on **any one** of the following. [20]

(i) Write an original short story starting with the words "Karan's exams were over and he was eagerly looking forward to the holidays. Suddenly, the doorbell rang and .... "

(ii) 'Children's opinion should be considered on matters concerning them.' Express your views for or against this statement.

(iii) During summer vacations, your family planned to go to Uttarakhand, the beautiful state. Your mother's first request was to visit Haridwar and Rishikesh before visiting any other place in the state. Narrate your visit to these holy places and share your experience in these twin holy cities.

(iv) Few months back, you lost your mother. You miss her every day and wish she were here with you. Write down your feelings and pleasant memories of your mother.

(v) Study the picture given below. Write a story or a description or an account of what the picture suggests to you. Your composition may be about the subject of the picture or you may take suggestions from it but there must be a clear connection between the picture and your composition.

Question 2.

(Do not spend more than 20 minutes on this question.)

Select **any one** of the following. [10]

(i) You are studying in a boarding school and your first mid-term exam results have shown that you have done poorly in two subjects, Maths and Science. Write a letter to your father explaining the reasons for your poor result. Also, write how you plan to do better in the term end exams as well as the Board exams next March.

(ii) Write a letter to the Municipal Commissioner of your city drawing his attention to the problems created by various hawkers of food outside your school gate. Tell him what dangers to the health of students they pose. Suggest a solution for their rehabilitation.

Question 3.

(i) You are Rohan/Roma, the Students' Representative of the School Development Committee. Next week, the Committee is meeting to prepare a Calendar of Activities for academic year 20XX-20XY. Write a notice to be put up on your school notice board inviting students' suggestions on the subject. [5]

(ii) Write an e-mail to Sunita Jalan, a business executive of Be the Best Group requesting her to sponsor a creative writing workshop as suggested in the Student Development Committee meeting. [5]

Question 4.

Read the following passage carefully and answer the questions that follow.

They pass me every day, on their way to school - boys and girls from the surrounding villages and the outskirts of the hill station. There are no school buses for these children : they walk. For many of them, it's a very long walk to school.

Ranbir, who is ten, has to climb the mountain from his village, four miles distant and two thousand feet below the town level. He comes in all kinds of weathers wearing the same pair of cheap shoes until they have almost fallen apart.

Ranbir is a cheerful soul. He waves to me whenever he sees me at my window.

Sometimes, he brings me cucumbers from his father's field. I pay him for the cucumbers; he uses the money for books or for small things needed at home.

Many of the children are like Ranbir - poor, but slightly better off than how their parents were at the same age. They cannot attend the expensive residential and private schools that abound here but must go to the government-aided schools with only basic facilities. Not many of their parents managed to go to school.

They spent their lives working in the fields or delivering milk in the hill station. The lucky ones got into the army. Perhaps, Ranbir will do something different when he grows up. He has yet to see a train but he sees planes flying over the mountains almost every day.

"How far can a plane go?", he asks.

"All over the world", I tell him. "Thousands of miles in a day, you can go almost anywhere."

"I'll go round the world one day" he vows. "I'll buy a plane and go everywhere!"

And, maybe he will. He has a determined chin and a **defiant** look in his eye. Up to a few years ago, very few girls in the hills or in the villages of India went to school. They helped in the home until they were old enough to be married which wasn't very old. But there are now just as many girls as there are boys going to school.

Bindra is something of an extrovert, a confident fourteen-year-old who chatters away as she hurries down the road with her companions. Her father is a forest guard and knows me quite well. I meet him on my walks through the deodar woods behind Landour. And I had grown used to seeing Bindra almost every day. When she did not put in an appearance for a week, I asked her brother if anything was wrong. "Oh, nothing," he says, "she is helping my mother cut grass. Soon, the monsoon will end and the grass will dry up. So, we cut it now and store it for the cows in winter."

"And why aren't you cutting grass too?"

"Oh, I have a cricket match today" he says, and hurries away to join his teammates. Unlike his sister, he puts pleasure before work! Cricket, once the game of the **elite**, has become the game of the masses. On any holiday, in any part of this vast country, groups of boys can be seen making their way to the nearest field, or open patch of land, with bat, ball and any other cricketing gear that they can cobble together. Watching some of them play, I am amazed at the quality of talent, at the finesse with which they bat or bowl.

Some of the local teams are as good if not better than any from the private schools where there are better facilities. But boys from these poor or lower middle-class families will never get the exposure that is necessary to bring them to the attention of those who select state or national teams. They will never get near enough to the men of influence and power. They must continue to play for the love of the game or watch their more fortunate heroes' exploits on television.

SP-01

(i) For each word given below, choose the correct meaning (as used in the passage) from the options provided. [2]

(1) *defiant* (line 21)

(a) the act of being rebellious
(b) to be compliant
(c) to be cooperative
(d) to be tractable

(2) *elite* (line 34)

(a) middle class
(b) upper or high class
(c) proletariat
(d) the masses

(ii) Which word in the passage means the opposite of the word 'ineptness'? [1]

(a) finesse
(b) influence
(c) exposure
(d) fortunate

(iii) Answer the following questions briefly in your own words.

(a) In what way are children better off than their parents? [2]

(b) Why does the author call the heroes on television 'fortunate'? [2]

(c) How has the fate of girls changed? [2]

(d) In what way was her brother different from Bindra? [2]

(e) What was Ranbir's ambition? [1]

(iv) In not more than 50 words, relate the difficulties that the children face in their daily lives. [8]

Question 5.

(i) Fill in each of the numbered blanks with correct form of the words given in brackets. Do not copy the passage but write in correct serial order the word or phrase appropriate to the blank space. [4]

Example : He ......(0)......(go) to London next week.

Answer: (0) is going/will go

The world's most famous clock, Big Ben, stands next to the Houses of Parliament in London. Big Ben is the name of the bell which ......**(1)**...... (chime) every hour. The bell ......**(2)**...... (name) after Sir Benjamin Hall, the man who ......**(3)**...... (give) the task of ......**(4)**...... (haul) the bell up the clock tower. The clock has four faces and ......**(5)**...... (keep) accurate time. It can ......**(6)**......(adjust) by the removal or addition of coins on a tray ......**(7)**...... (attach) to the clock's pendulum.

One interesting thing about the clock is that when the light ......**(8)**...... (shine) above the belfry at night, it means that the house of commons is still in session.

(ii) Fill in each blank with an appropriate word. [4]

(a) After the train left, it started to rain. So, I took shelter ...... the station.

(b) I have got ...... the train and will reach Bengaluru by 6 pm.

(c) You should not look directly at the Sun ...... an eclipse.

(d) I saw the dog scrambling ...... the road.

(e) I went to see him ...... at the station

(f) You have to bring my car back ...... the end of the month.

(g) There are plenty of fish ...... this pond.

(h) The book fair is open ...... 5th April.

SP-01 (iii) Join the following sentences to make one complete sentence **without using and, but** or **so.** Choose the correct option. [4]

(1) She is hard working. She is not intelligent.

(a) Despite being hard working, she is not intelligent.

(b) Despite of being hard working, she is not hard working.

(c) Despite of being intelligent, she is not hard working.

(d) Despite being intelligent, she is hard working.

(2) He is greedy. He is dishonest.

(a) He is greedy but dishonest.

(b) He is greedy otherwise dishonest.

(c) He is greedy as well as dishonest.

(d) He is greedy moreover dishonest.

(3) She had the qualifications. She did not get the job.

(a) Although she had the qualifications, but she did not get the job.

(b) Although she had the qualifications, yet she did not get the job.

(c) Although she had the qualifications, yet she got the job.

(d) Although she had the qualifications, she did not get the job.

(4) I tried to look happy. I felt miserable.
(a) I tried to look happy in spite feeling miserable.
(b) I tried to look happy despite felt miserable.
(c) I tried to look happy despite of feeling miserable.
(d) I tried to look happy in spite of feeling miserable.

(iv) Choose the correct option to rewrite the following according to the instructions given after each sentence. [8]

(1) Not many people like politicians these days.
[Rewrite beginning with : Few]
(a) Few people do not like politicians these days.
(b) Few people like politicians these days.
(c) Few people does not like politicians these days.
(d) Few people do like politicians these days.

(2) She had a lot of books but she was not educated.
[Begin with : In spite]
(a) In spite having a lot of books, she was educated.
(b) In spite of having a lot of books, she was educated.
(c) In spite of having a lot of books, she was not educated.
(d) In spite having a lot of books, she was not educated.

(3) As soon as I started for the office, it began to rain.
[Begin with : Hardly]
(a) Hardly had I started for the office when it began to rain.
(b) Hardly had I started for the office than it began to rain.
(c) Hardly did I started for the office when it began to rain.
(d) Hardly did I start for the office than it began to rain.

(4) You are so confused that you cannot choose.
[Rewrite using : too ... to..]
(a) You are too confused to choose. (b) You are too confused to not choose.
(c) You are not too confused to choose. (d) None of these

(5) Each one of these girls is very smart.
[Use : dull]
(a) There is every girl who can be termed 'dull'. (b) Every girl can be termed 'dull'.
(c) There is no girl that can be termed 'dull'. (d) None of these

(6) It is harmful and unhealthy to eat junk food.
[Begin with : It is not ...]
(a) It is not useful and unhealthy to eat junk food.
(b) It is not useless and healthy to eat junk food.
(c) It is not useless and unhealthy to eat junk food.
(d) It is not useful and healthy to eat junk food.

(7) Who had started the fight?
[Rewrite using passive voice]
(a) By whom was the fight started? (b) By whom had the fight been started?
(c) By whom has the fight been started? (d) All of these

(8) He said, 'Burglars broke into my house last night.'
[Rewrite using indirect speech]
(a) He said that burglars have broken into his house the last night.
(b) He said that burglars had broken into his house the previous night.
(c) He said that burglars broke into his house the last night.
(d) He said that burglars broken into his house the previous night.

Answers in Topper's Style

1. (i) Karan's exams were over and he was eagerly looking forward to the holidays. Suddenly, the doorbell rang and one of his cousins named Mahesh, who was known to be very careless and destructive, entered. He announced, "Karan, I have come to stay here for the holidays." In the process, he jumped on to Karan's bed and damaged his crayon box. Karan was now sure his holidays were going to be ruined.

They switched on the TV in the evening. In the middle of a news programme, an announcement was made that a convicted murderer had escaped from the local jail. A photograph of the criminal was displayed. The announcer cautioned all persons to take precautions that night to ensure that the murderer did not enter any of their homes. Karan secured all doors and windows before they went to sleep in one room as Karan's parents were not home.

Suddenly, he was awakened by some noises coming from the dining room. When he peeped out of the door of his room, he saw an unknown person with a torch entering through a broken window. Obviously, it was a burglar. So, he quietly woke up Mahesh and told him to remain quiet till they decided the plan of action.

Meanwhile, the burglar had entered his parents' bedroom where all of his mother's jewellery was kept. He told Mahesh to rush and bolt the room's door from outside. Simultaneously, he went to the landline telephone in the drawing room and quickly dialled the police to come and arrest the burglar.

While they waited for the police to turn up, the burglar started banging his parents' bedroom door from the inside. When he realised that the door was bolted from the outside, he ran to the window to escape by breaking it open. But, he did not succeed because of the steel grill put on the window. Eventually, the police arrived and arrested the burglar after unbolting the door.

Thus, due to Mahesh's presence in the house, Karan's holidays had not been ruined. In fact, Mahesh played a key role in nabbing the criminal and made him smile with happiness.

(ii)

For the Motion

Children are the future of the world so their opinions must be considered when taking a decision concerning them. There are thousands of kids expressing their opinions and protesting, to try and change the world. We must learn to respect our children's opinion because children express who they are and do what they want. They will grow up to become doctors, lawyers, singers and so much more so in my opinion, their opinions do matter!

This can be illustrated by a recent real life incident in the USA. A maniacal armed gunman shot and killed a number of children at a school in front of other students. The trauma was so much that about 100 of these teenage students travelled 650 km to the state capital just to protest against the liberal gun laws in that country. They were absolutely within their rights to demand change in the laws.

Children and their opinions should not be ignored as age is not a criteria of emotional or mental maturity. Thinking that only people above 18 years of age are mature is incorrect as, even though they might legally not be considered an adult, children are still people with their own thoughts and ideas. To not consider their opinions would be to not give them their Right to Freedom of Expression.

Although there are certain rules made for a child's benefit such as no alcoholic drinks for people below 25 years, no driving of motorised vehicles for people below 16 years, etc., the restriction should not extend to all areas. We all know that Sachin Tendulkar represented India at the age of 16 and even some of our current champion rifle shooters are below 14 years. Thus, there should not be an age restriction on children for expressing their opinion on matters concerning them.

Against the Motion

Children are considered immature personalities as they have neither completed their education, nor have adequate experience of day-to-day matters to give a sound opinion on any matter even those that concern them. As a result, they depend on the opinion of their elders and form opinion to their like and dislike.

Children tend to forget that the adults were once the same age as they are now. But now, the adults have more experience. All adults are aware that children and teenagers tend to have foolish and impractical ideas due to their incomplete knowledge or lack of experience. For instance, one child felt that having shorter school days and longer summer breaks will improve their grades as they will have to study less and consequently do better. Today's enlightened generation of children expects the government to provide everything but they forget that the money for everything comes from taxes. So, if government needs more money, it will impose higher taxes. Thus, the reality is that children are immature.

In addition, children can be very easily manipulated. What you hear as their opinion is probably not their own. They don't think for themselves. Most children only repeat what their parents say to them. Although children are smarter than most adults think, they are very easily influenced by people who they think are 'good' or 'ideal'.

Children's minds are so open that they are prone to accepting anything a credible adult teaches them as the truth. When children argue for a cause, their 'opinions' are usually words that an adult has put into their head. Someone can easily manipulate a child into saying words that are not their own and, if we take it as important, we are disrespecting the true opinions of a population.

Thus, it is clear that children's opinions on matters, even those that concern them, need not be considered.

(iii) During my summer vacations, my father planned a visit to Uttarakhand. On my mother's request, we decided to visit holy towns near Roorkee on the banks of the river Ganga. On Saturday morning, we drove up to Haridwar, a distance of about 240 km from Delhi.

While entering Haridwar, we found a distinct change in the environment. There were a large number of temples. Devotees were crowding the temples as it was festive season. It appeared as if we were nearing heaven and God was everywhere. We drove straight to Har ki Pauri on the banks of the Ganga to have a ritual bath. As we were early, there was not much of a crowd there. After visiting various temples in the town, we had a hearty lunch in one of the restaurants nearby. In the afternoon, we visited the Mansa Devi temple by travelling in the cable car to the hilltop on which the temple is situated. In the cable car, it seemed as if I was a bird flying in the sky. When I looked down from it, the scenery and the view of the river Ganga were exquisite.

I immediately took some photos with the camera in my mobile phone. The temple itself was decorated tastefully. We decided to walk down the hill on our return which was an enjoyable exercise for me. We then rested at a hotel where we would be staying the night. In the evening, we watched the Ganga aarti at 7 p.m. which was a grand spectacle.

On Sunday, we went to Rishikesh which has a number of bridges across the river for devotees interested in visiting temples located there. They have picturesque names such as Lakshaman Jhula, Sivananda Jhula (also called Ram Jhula), etc. While crossing the first bridge, I was dropping food for the fish in the river. I saw the wonderful sight of the fish jumping out of water to grab the food morsels.

After having a lavish lunch at the famous Chotiwala restaurant, we moved ahead to other places including Uttarkashi and Badrinath. It was a memorable trip.

(iv) **My Mother**

Without any doubt, my mother was the most important person in my life and the most powerful individual I have ever known. She was very beautiful and had the kindest eyes that I have ever seen. She not only worked hard to ensure that I had a good upbringing but was also very strict and often punished me whenever I was wrong. Even though I did not like the punishment back then, I now look back and realise that it was meant to lovingly correct me and help me choose the right path while growing up.

My two sisters and I have always taken pride in the appearance of our mother, especially her lovely long hair. I remember whenever my mother came to visit us at our boarding school, other students would urge us to ask her to remove the pins from her hair so that they could see her long well-kept hair. One of the reasons that my sisters and I were especially fond of my mother is the way she used to take great care of us, especially when we were ill. She was a very knowledgeable lady who made a variety of home remedies to help take care of the minor illnesses that we had as children.

My sisters and I did not like to see our mother sad and would do just about anything to bring a smile to her face. Interestingly, even when she was very worried or sad about something, she would always smile to make us stop worrying for her. My mother not only loved those around her but was also compassionate towards strangers. We often observed her compassion towards our neighbours, especially when a new neighbour moved in or when one of the neighbours was going through a hard time. My mother would sacrifice her time to go to a needy neighbour with a hot bowl of soup that would instantly make the neighbour feel appreciated.

My mother was a good cook which always left us looking forward to the next meal. She knew how to mix the right ingredients to end up with a meal that often left us licking our fingers. Just the memory of the foods that my mother prepared for us makes me salivate to this present day. I miss her very much and wish she were here for a longer period of time.

(v) **A Ride on a Giant Wheel**

The picture shows a giant wheel which has fascinated people of all age group for a long time. Most people eagerly go for rides on giant wheels on which they are tossed in the air just as vegetables in a mixer-grinder. At some point in history, someone thought that people would enjoy rides on such a machine and that person invented what must have been the first of these giant wheels. For me, it is the thrill and excitement of having survived the ride that has me coming back for more.

My first experience with such a ride was at a local fair. Looking at that huge wheel whirling round and round, I was thrilled. It was huge, noisy and somewhat intimidating. Ever since that initial impression was frozen in my imagination many years ago, the droning sound of their engines brings to mind the great roar of a fire-breathing dragon with smoke spewing from its exhaust-pipe nostrils. The first ride on one of these giant wheels gave me an instant thrill. I sat with two other passengers in one of the carriages. We were strapped inside and soon the wheel started to rotate slowly. As the wheel gained speed, the resistance to gravity built up against my body until I was unable to move.

As my carriage reached the top of its climb, my body relaxed. Then, suddenly my stomach churned as I felt weightless as we went down. A crashing sound vibrated through the air as the wheel reached bottom and, much to my surprise, we began to rise again.

Each new rotation gave me more confidence in the giant wheel. Every ascent left me elated that I had survived the previous death-defying fall. When another nerve-wracking climb failed to follow the last exhilarating descent, the ride was over. I then realised that I had enjoyed the ride. Physically and emotionally drained, I followed my fellow passengers down the metal steps to reach the safety of the ground. A trip on the wonderful giant wheel never fails to thrill me. Although I am becoming older and have less time, or less inclination, to ride them, I still do so if I am given the opportunity.

2. (i) St. Xavier School,
Gandhi Maidan,
Patna – 800001

17th July, 20XX

Dear Papa,

I understand that you must be upset with my mid-term exam report which you must have received by now. I regret my poor performance in both Maths and Science. I feel depressed at having let you down, especially after you spent so much time in helping me complete my holiday homework during the summer.

I do not want to make any excuses but, as you know, I had an attack of malaria two weeks ago and was unable to attend classes for about a week. Then, the mid-term exams were held which caught me unprepared. That is why I scored very poorly in these subjects.

I have now fully recovered and am fit to study intensively. I have requested my Maths and Science teachers to give me some extra time to understand some basic concepts in these subjects. I also plan to study in a group with some of the other students.

I am sure that this will help me to score much better marks in the term-end exams and finally in the Board exams next year.

Please do not be worried about my health as I am much better now. I look forward to meeting you during the Diwali holidays.

Yours affectionately,
Sanjeev

(ii) 12/ C, Kaiser Ganj Road,
Meerut - 250002

19th August, 20XX

The Municipal Commissioner,
Meerut Nagar Nigam,
Meerut - 250002

Dear Sir/Ma'am,

As the Secretary of Swachh Bharat Club, St. Francis Convent School, I wish to draw your attention to the menace of hawkers outside our school situated in Kanker Khera on Sardhana Road.

The hawkers cook and sell popular snack items on the road outside our school without taking care of cleanliness. A number of students cluster around them during the lunch break and after school gets over. The hawkers do not keep wastebaskets, nor do they maintain cleanliness; consequently, flies and other insects hover continuously over the food items.

I request you to look into this problem urgently so that the health of our students does not deteriorate. The hawkers must be warned about the importance of maintaining hygiene and the sale of clean food. They must also be licensed by the Corporation to ensure that they follow all the regulations. I also suggest that they may be shifted to any open space nearby so that the road in front of the school remains free for passage of traffic. This would ensure that they are not deprived of their livelihood and the area in front of our school is kept clean and congestion free.

I trust that you will consider my suggestion and take the steps required to ensure 'Swachh Bharat'.

Thanking you,

Yours sincerely,
Mayank Sinha
(Secretary, Swachh Bharat Club)
St. Francis Convent School

3. (i)

Annual Development Committee Meeting

Date: Wednesday, 31st March, 20XX
Time: 9 a.m. to 1 p.m.
Venue: Study Hall, Room 305

The purpose of the meet is to create a calendar of activities for the coming session. Members are requested to come with suggestions.

(ii) To: p_ jalan147@yahoo.co.in

Subject Request to sponsor creative writing workshop

Dear Ma'am,

This is to inform you that we, the Student Development Committee, have written this mail to request you to sponsor our creative writing workshop.

Your educational firm, Be the Best, has shown remarkable growth in the field of content development. We feel that, with your support, we can enrich our students with good and practical skills. Hoping for your positive reply.

Thanking you,

Yours faithfully,
Sam Matthew
President, Student Development Committee

4. (i) (1) (a) the act of being rebellious

(2) (b) upper or high class

(ii) (a) finesse

(iii) (a) Children are better off than their parents because they get a chance to attend a government-aided school with basic facilities. Many parents could not go to school as they spent their lives working in the fields or delivering milk in the hill station.

(b) The author calls the heroes on television 'fortunate' because they get name and fame, besides a lot of money. Thus, they can lead an influential and powerful life.

(c) The fate of girls has changed because they also go to school instead of helping with household work all the time. They are now getting a chance to lead a better life.

(d) Bindra's brother was different from her as he was given more freedom. He could play cricket or enjoy with friends instead of having to cut grass or work at home.

(e) Ranbir's ambition was to buy a plane one day and go round the world.

(iv) The children living in remote areas face many difficulties due to lack of school buses such as walking long distances, including climbing hills, walking without shoes during rainy season. Girls now attend the school on regular basis and yet, when it comes to helping in household or field work, they are the ones found helping their mothers and not the boys.

5. (1) chimes (2) was named (3) was given (4) hauling
(5) keeps (6) be adjusted (7) attached (8) shines

(ii) (a) at (b) on (c) during (d) across
(e) off (f) by (g) in (h) until

(iii) (1) (a) Despite being hard working, she is not intelligent.
(2) (c) He is greedy as well as dishonest.
(3) (d) Although she had the qualifications, she did not get the job.
(4) (d) I tried to look happy in spite of feeling miserable.

(iv) (1) (b) Few people like politicians these days.
(2) (c) In spite of having a lot of books, she was not educated.
(3) (a) Hardly had I started for the office when it began to rain.
(4) (a) You are too confused to choose.
(5) (c) There is no girl that can be termed 'dull'.
(6) (d) It is not useful and healthy to eat junk food.
(7) (b) By whom had the fight been started?
(8) (b) He said that burglars had broken into his house the previous night.

SQP Code : **PB-2/10** Series ***i*-Succeed 2-25/10** Roll No. | | | | | | | | |

Sample Question Paper 02

English Language 10th (Code 01)

General Instructions

1. You will not be allowed to write during the first 15 minutes. This time is to be spent in reading the question paper.
2. The time given at the head of this paper is the time allowed for writing the answers.
3. Attempt all five questions.
4. The intended marks for questions or parts of questions are given in brackets [].
5. You are advised to spend not more than 30 minutes in answering Question 1 and 20 minutes in answering Question 2.

Time : 2 Hrs.

Max. Marks : 80

Question 1.

(Do not spend more than 30 minutes on this question.)

Write a composition (300-350 words) on **any one** of the following. [20]

(i) Write an original short story entitled 'Ghost in the Storm!'

(ii) 'All girls or all boys schools provide a better learning environment than co-educational schools.' Express your views either for or against the statement.

(iii) You are fond of reading books and always look for opportunities to explore new reading experiences. Recently, a 'World Book Fair' was held at Pragati Maidan in New Delhi. Describe your visit and share the experience you had at this book fair.

(iv) "Fast food may tickle our taste buds, but it harms our health in more ways than we can count." When fast food fanatic Gauri Shankar heard her doctor says these words, she was horrified and immediately decided to quit fast food. She even took on the responsibility of spreading awareness about the harmful effects of fast food.

Write a composition for her to be printed in the school magazine on the topic 'Junk This Food'.

(v) Study the picture given below. Write a story or a description or an account of what it suggests to you. Your composition may be about the subject of the picture or you may take suggestions from it. However, there must be a clear connection between the picture and your composition.

Question 2.

(Do not spend more than 20 minutes on it.)

Select **any one** of the following. [10]

(i) You are Kavita Yadav, a resident of B–3/13 Ashok Vihar, New Delhi. You have noticed that, in spite of the government's initiatives and provisions made for the girl child, the actual school enrolment statistics do not show an encouraging trend. Write a letter to the Editor of a national daily expressing your concern about the issue and the need to work on a war footing to counter the problem of poor enrolment of girls.

(ii) Write a letter to your friend 'Pawan' apologising for your thoughtlessness about revealing his business secrets to someone else. You are Kunal Goswami.

Question 3.

(i) Your school is organising a donation drive for the underprivileged children of the slum areas near your school. As the Head Girl of your school, write a notice for your school notice board informing students about the event and inviting them to donate whatever they can to make the donation drive a success. [5]

(ii) Write an e-mail to the Principal of a nearby school requesting him to allow the students of his school to participate in the donation drive. [5]

Question 4.

Read the following passage carefully and answer the questions that follow.

We have been brought up to fear insects. We regard them as unnecessary creatures that do more harm than good. Man continuously wages war on them for they contaminate his food, carry diseases or devour his crops. They sting or bite without provocation, they fly uninvited into our rooms on summer nights or beat against our lighted windows. We live in dread not only of unpleasant insects such as spiders or wasps but of quite harmless ones such as moths. Reading about them increases our understanding without **dispelling** our fears. Knowing that the industrious ants live in a highly organised society does not prevent us from being filled with revulsion when we find hordes of them crawling over a carefully prepared picnic lunch.

No matter how much we like honey or how much we have read of the uncanny sense of direction which bees possess, we have a horror of being stung. Most of our fears are unreasonable but they are difficult to erase. At the same time, however, insects are strangely fascinating. We enjoy reading about them, especially when we find that as the Praying Mantis, they lead perfectly horrible lives. We enjoy staring at them, entranced as they go about their business, unaware-we hope-of our presence. Who has not stood in awe at the sight of a spider **pouncing** on a fly or a column of ants triumphantly carrying home an enormous dead beetle? Last summer, I spent many days in the garden watching thousands of ants crawling up the trunk of my prized peach tree. The tree has grown against a warm wall on a sheltered side of the house. I am especially proud of it not only because it has survived several severe winters but also because it occasionally produces luscious peaches. During the summer, I noticed that the leaves of the tree had begun to wither. Clusters of tiny insects called Aphids were to be found on the underside of the leaves. They were visited by a large column of ants which obtained a sort of honey from them. I immediately embarked on an experiment which, even though it failed to get rid of the ants, kept me fascinated for twenty four hours. I bound the base of the tree with sticky tape, making it impossible for the ants to reach the Aphids. The tape was so sticky that they did not dare to cross it. For a long time, I watched them scurrying around the base of the tree in bewilderment. I even went out at midnight with a torch and noted with satisfaction and surprise that the ants were still swarming around the sticky tape without being able to do anything about it. I got up early next morning to find the ants were climbing up the wall of the house and then on to the leaves of the tree. I realised sadly that I had been completely defeated by their ingenuity. The ants had been quick to find an answer to my thoroughly unscientific methods.

(i) For each word given below, choose the correct mean (as used in the passage) from the options provided. [2]

(1) *dispelling* (line 6)

(a) engendering (b) getting rid of

(c) producing something (d) causing an effect

(2) *pouncing* (line 16)

(a) moving suddenly to attack or capture (b) dropping dead

(c) walking slowly and calmly (d) staying very still

(ii) Which word in the passage means the opposite of the word 'stupidity'? [1]

(a) Provocation (b) Revulsion

(c) Ingenuity (d) Bewilderment

(iii) Answer the following questions briefly in your own words.

(a) What is our attitude towards insects? [2]

(b) Why does man try to exterminate insects? [2]

(c) What did the writer do to prevent the ants from reaching the Aphids? Was it successful? [2]

(d) Why does the writer say that knowing about insects does not make man change his attitude towards them? [2]

(e) What was the reason that the leaves of the tree were beginning to wither in summer? [1]

(iv) In not more than 50 words, describe the behaviour that we show towards insects. [8]

Question 5.

(i) Fill in each of the numbered blanks with correct form of the words given in brackets. Do not copy the passage but write in correct serial order the word or phrase appropriate to the blank space. [4]

Example You should ....**(0)**......... (call) me before.

Answer (0) have called

It is not unusual for all sorts of insects to be called bugs. However, in reality, this name should only ...**(1)**... (give) to a particular group of insects called Hemipetra.

These insects have tube-like beaks which they use to ...**(2)**... (suck) sap from the plants on which they ...**(3)**... (live). Others prey upon other insects by ...**(4)**... (inject) poison into them.

These insects are brightly ...**(5)**... (colour) and come in all sizes and shapes.

A nymph, or a young bug, has no wings and cannot ...**(6)**... (fly). Adult bugs, however, ...**(7)**... (have) two pairs of wings. When not in use, the hind pair of wings ...**(8)**... (lie) folded and hidden behind the front pair.

(ii) Fill in each blank with an appropriate word. [4]

(a) There were fifty rooms ...... the hotel.

(b) I play cricket .... the Lion's Cricket Club every weekend.

(c) The flight was fine but the food ...... the plane wasn't good.

(d) I first saw the newly-launched phone in the shop .... MG Road.

(e) I waited for my friend .... 5 p.m. but he didn't turn up.

(f) My friend didn't turn up even .... 5 p.m.

(g) I somehow made it .... the road unscathed despite so much traffic.

(h) I visited most places of tourist interest .... my stay in Paris.

(iii) Join the following sentences to make one complete sentence **without using and, but** or **so**. Choose the correct option. [4]

(1) My sister works three jobs in a day. She doesn't earn much money.

(a) My sister works three jobs in a day; nonetheless, she doesn't earn much money.

(b) My sister works three jobs in a day; however, she doesn't earn much money.

(c) My sister works three jobs in a day; consequently, she doesn't earn much money.

(d) My sister works three jobs in a day; otherwise, she doesn't earn much money.

(2) We went out. The weather was cold.

(a) We went out despite of the cold weather.

(b) We went out despite the cold weather.

(c) We went out in spite the cold weather.

(d) None of the above

(3) He was ill. He attended the meeting.

(a) Though he was ill, yet he attended the meeting.

(b) Though he was ill, but he attended the meeting.

(c) Though he was ill; however, he attended the meeting.

(d) Though he was ill, he attended the meeting.

(4) She is pretty. She is intelligent.

(a) She is pretty and she is intelligent.

(b) She is pretty or intelligent.

(c) She is neither pretty nor intelligent.

(d) She is pretty as well as intelligent.

(iv) Choose the correct option to rewrite the following according to instructions given after each sentence. [8]

(1) Passing examinations is a goal. Every candidate should aim at it.
[Rewrite using : to]

(a) Every candidate should aim to pass the examination.

(b) Every candidate should aim to passing the examination.

(c) Every candidate should aiming to pass the examination.

(d) None of the above

(2) If you gave me fifty thousand Kenya Shillings, I would not go down a coal mine.
[Rewrite using : even if]

(a) Even if I would not go down a coal mine, you gave me fifty thousand Kenya shillings.

(b) Even if you gave me fifty thousand Kenya shillings, I would go down a coal mine.

(c) I would go down a coal mine even if you gave me fifty thousand Kenya shillings.

(d) None of the above

(3) As soon as he got onto the bus, the driver started the engine.
[Begin with : No sooner .....]
(a) No sooner did he get on the bus, the driver started the engine.
(b) No sooner did he get on the bus than the driver started the engine.
(c) No sooner had he get on the bus than the driver started the engine.
(d) No sooner had he get on the bus the driver started the engine.

(4) If he apologises, he will be pardoned.
[Use : unless]
(a) He will be pardoned unless he apologises.
(b) He will not be pardoned unless he apologies.
(c) Unless he will not be pardoned, he apologies.
(d) Unless he will be pardoned, he apologises.

(5) The sheep ate a lot.
[Begin with : A lot]
(a) A lot was eaten by the sheep.
(b) A lot is eaten by the sheep.
(c) A lot had been eaten by the sheep.
(d) A lot is beeing eaten by the sheep.

(6) Did Sue draw this circle?
[Begin with : Was]
(a) Was this circle draw by Sue?
(b) Was this circle drew by Sue?
(c) Was this circle being drawn by Sue?
(d) Was this circle drawn by Sue?

(7) There is no success without effort.
[Begin with : Whenever ....]
(a) Whenever there is no effort, there is success.
(b) Whenever there is effort, there is no success.
(c) Whenever there is effort, there is success.
(d) None of the above

(8) He said, 'I am writing a letter.'
[Begin with : He said that...]
(a) He said that he is writing a letter.
(b) He said that he was writing a letter.
(c) He said that a letter was written by him.
(d) He said that a letter was being written by him.

Answers *in Topper's Style*

1. (i)

Ghost in the Storm

There was a violent storm blowing outside at 9 pm. My brother and I were all alone at home. We were living in a quite secluded region. Any other house was at a far distance. Suddenly, the lights went out which caused total darkness in our house because we had not installed an inverter. As we sat waiting for the electric supply to be restored, a strange sound came from outside the front door which scared the daylights out of me. I was afraid to open the door so I told my younger brother, Vicky to find out who it was. But, Vicky himself had jumped in fright at the sound and did not move. Finally, I mustered enough courage to go and open the door. I screamed in horror at what I saw! There was a ghostly apparition standing there, shaking. I ran back to my room and shut the door.

For sometime, only the howling of the storm was heard. Then, to my relief, the lights came back.

I opened my door and switched on the porch light from inside the house. When I looked again, I saw my father standing there in a white kurta pyjama with a white cap. I rushed to the porch and hugged my father in relief. Just imagine, I had mistaken him for an apparition! Immediately, I apologised to him for not recognising him and asked Vicky to come out to meet him.

My father had walked to the nearby market to get some medicines and was walking back when the storm broke. He stood under a tree to wait but got wet from head to toe due to the intensity of the rain.

This caused him to shiver uncontrollably. He already had a very sore throat and could not speak easily. So, we brought him inside and made him change into dry clothes before putting him into bed for the night.

The next morning, when he had recovered somewhat, we all had a hearty laugh at how I had mistaken him to be a ghost last night.

(ii) **For the Motion**

It has been noted that an all-girls or all-boys school can provide a more structured learning environment for both girls and boys, respectively. Boys and girls differ in the way they act, how they learn, and their interests and abilities. They need an educational environment tailored to meet their unique needs. In general, boys are more physically active, assertive and comfortable learning in a more chaotic environment than girls.

Girls are able to sit still and prefer a quiet, focused and orderly classroom. In all-girls or all-boys schools, the curriculum and course provide advanced work in areas of the children's greatest interests and natural abilities.

Moreover, single-sex schools encourage children to take risks in expressing themselves as they learn without the fear of embarrassing themselves in front of the opposite sex. Without boys in their classes, girls are more likely to be leaders and reach higher levels of achievement which leads to greater self-confidence and higher professional aspirations. In the secondary and senior secondary classes, single-sex schools remove the distraction of the opposite sex, allowing students to focus more seriously on their schoolwork.

A study conducted states that single-sex schools develop greater self-confidence and broader interests especially among adolescents. Girls report that they feel more comfortable; they can interact more with teachers and develop a more favourable attitude towards subjects such as maths and science.

In addition, schools for boys allow adequate time for male maturation and benefit them by giving them more structure and discipline due to their tendencies of restlessness and aggression. Furthermore, separating girls and boys fosters an environment of non-stereotyping and encourages learning. It also promotes interest for boys in humanities course and they feel more at ease. It benefits girls as co-educational schools foster obsession over hair and clothes which tends to keep them distracted.

The students in all-girls or all-boys schools also feel the freedom to attend classes usually associated with the opposite sex, such as in the subject biology. Thus, in my opinion, all girls and all boys schools provide a better learning environment than co-educational schools.

Against the Motion

Co-education and its benefits for long has been a topic of debate in our country. Education in general sense is a form of learning in which the knowledge, skills, values and beliefs are transferred from the teacher to his disciples.

The modes of education do not vary as per the sex of the students. Thus, education cannot be divided on the lines of sex. When it comes to schools, there are many more important issues than having same sex schools. In fact, the age-old belief of same sex schools being better than co-educational schools has been long dismissed by the impressive results of the latter. Not only have the students of co-educational schools done academically well but it has also been seen that they are more confident than the students of same sex schools.

When girls sit along with boys in the same classroom, it helps develop a cordial relation among students and instils in them a spirit of sportsmanship, mutual harmony and brotherhood. Moreover, co-ed schools offer a diverse curriculum that is available to all students de-emphasising gender-linked stereotypes related to course work. Co-ed schools encourage all children to explore a broad range of banning opportunities. Today is an age where men and women work together and compete with each other in offices, homes, etc.; thus, co-education teaches and prepares them to interact with the opposite sex in the future.

Boys and girls learn to respect one another and cooperate as equals. As such, this system of study helps both the boys and girls to improve their confidence and also provides for an excellent foundation in developing realistic and meaningful relationships.

(iii) I am very fond of reading books. I look for opportunities to explore new books everyday. Book fair always attract me. A number of such fairs are organised by the National Book Trust on a regular basis at Pragati Maidan in New Delhi. Out of these, the World Book Fair is the largest as famous and reputed publishers from all across the world participate in it. It is organised every alternate year.

When we were informed that our class would visit this fair next Saturday, we were overjoyed. Our class teacher accompanied us to the fair. We were told that we had to be in uniform and also had to carry our identity cards. Then, we would not need any entry tickets.

On Saturday, we reached school at the usual time. From there we sat in the school bus which would take us to Pragati Maidan. We reached there at 10 o'clock. When we entered, we observed that each hall was segmented into many stalls managed by the respective publishing houses.

There were local publishers, national publishers and international publishers. There were attractive hoardings everywhere and signboards to guide us to wherever we wanted to go. Security arrangements were strictly followed. We had to pass through metal detectors to enter each of the halls. Our teacher first took all of us in a group to the biggest hall which housed the stalls of Indian publishers of school books. There, we found that every publisher had his own method to attract the students and interested visitors to his stall. Some were offering heavy discounts whereas others were offering gifts on every purchase. Some publishers had made a special seating arrangement for the readers who wanted to browse through the books on display.

Then, we visited the other halls in the fair. They displayed children's books, subject-oriented books, books on language and literature, books on performing arts, science and technology, books on software and hardware, banking and finance, management and accounting, medicine, law, cookery, health, beauty and fitness as well as famous literary classics. In addition, there was a huge collection of dictionaries.

I bought many books of my choice. We had snacks in a cafeteria inside Pragati Maidan. Soon, it was time to return. It had been an enjoyable day.

(iv)

Junk This Food

by Gauri Shankar

Fast food is the food served commercially which takes a short span to cook, is very tasty and affordable. Junk food tastes good which is why it is mostly liked by people of any age group especially kids and school-going children. But, in an attempt to meet taste requirements at a low price, several nutritional compromises are made. According to the research by scientists, it has been found that junk food has negative effect on the health of people who consume it in a large quantity.

They are generally fried food or food high in cholesterol, sugar, sodium, additives and preservatives, each of which has been linked to the development of chronic degenerative disorders. It also contains low amount of protective components like fibre and antioxdiants.

Many fast foods have a wide variety of chemical additives used to preserve, emulsify, colour and enhance the products to ensure uniformity, taste and profitability. These may pose health risks. Monosodium Glutamate (MSG), for example, is often used as a flavour enhancer and can lead to headaches, tightness in the chest and a burning sensation in the forearms and back of the neck.

Processed and junk foods are the means of rapid and unhealthy weight gain. Some foods like french fries, pizzas, burgers, candy, soft drinks, cookies, etc. are fine examples of high sugar and high fat containing items. Eating more junk food daily leads to nutritional deficiencies in the body because it lacks essential nutrients, vitamins, iron, minerals and dietary fibres. It increases risk of cardiovascular diseases because it is rich in saturated fat, sodium and bad cholesterol. Junk food also contains high level of carbohydrate which spikes blood sugar level and makes a person more lethargic, sleepy, and less active and alert.

While consuming more junk food, we lose out on the fibre, vitamins, minerals and other protective foods. So be careful in future when you have craving for fast food. Think about its harmful effect and try to eat fresh cooked food and fruits to maintain a good health.

(v) The given picture is of a popcorn seller who used to sell popcorns in my locality. 'Dignity of life lies in the dignity of labour; The popcornwalla used to quote this proverb often whenever I met him on the street.
His name is Lalit Narayan–a young smiling face with an oath to fight against all kinds of adversities in the most enjoyable manner. I thought about his name for a long time and felt a deep touch of irony. He is 'Narayan', i.e. Lord Vishnu but, for all of us, he is a 'popcornwalla' selling popcorns everyday as usual.
A little peep into his life will tell you much about him. He was hardly ten years old when destiny chose to spite him mercilessly and threw him into a pool of misfortunes.

First, his father met with an accident and died after suffering miserably in the hospital for ten long months. His mother could not accept this injustice of God and fell ill. He loved his mother very much and nursed her day and night to see her walking again in the house and shouting angrily and loudly as before. He missed the valiant spirit of his mother. Everyday, he watched her slow and painful journey to death. But, even his blind devotion and love for his mother along with his tireless prayers to God could not save her. He lost her too.

Those were the days of his painful poverty and he had to fight against all odds with the only support of his life, his wife, Lalita. Probably, that was the moment that gave him strength to rise up and soon he stood up above everything-pain, misery, poverty, sickness and loneliness, all of which made him 'The Man'. Narayan, 'the Man' is, very happy and busy nowadays. He no more regrets or repents his past and never goes down memory lane to feel the hard punches of his misfortunes. He is 'destiny' himself marching ahead with his wife. He calls it his rebirth with the only target to enjoy life. He laughs a lot and always serves his customers with a broad smile. His tight routine demands ten hours work at a stretch but he willingly accepts it. He leads life with his wife as a willing companion who has submitted happily to every challenge in life. He has a great passion for his work and salutes life with jealous determination. After all, he is 'Lalit Narayan Popcornwalla'.

2. (i) B-3/13Ashok Vihar,
New Delhi 10054

7th March, 20XX

The Editor,
The Indian Express,
New Delhi - 110002

Subject Poor Enrolment of Girls in Schools

Dear Sir/Ma'am,

Through the column of your esteemed newspaper, I wish to throw light on the prevailing poor school enrolment ratio of girls in our country. Education is a human right enshrined in the Universal Declaration of Human Rights. Therefore, it is of utmost importance that education is given to all, regardless of any discrimination.

Gender discrimination and cultural factors continue to make the situation worse. Collective efforts on a war footing and on an individual and national level are needed now. Some parents hesitate to send girls to far off schools by raising their concern for security. Considering this, more educational institutions must be opened in safe and nearby areas. Awareness programmes should be conducted to sensitise parents as it is important for the poor to understand the importance of education. Incentives in the form of financial scholarships may also help motivate poor parents to enrol their girl child. With these steps, we may emancipate and empower girls of our country.

Thanking you,

Yours sincerely,
Kavita Yadav

(ii) 137, Granary Road,
Patna, Bihar

24th May, 20XX

Dear Pawan,

I hope everything is fine on your end.

I am writing this letter to apologise to you formally for my thoughtlessness and reckless behaviour. It was really foolish on my part to talk about you and your business secrets with someone else who is in the same business. Though my action was unintentional, it was reckless and immature and I am really sorry for that.

I realise that I have hurt you by this foolish act but I sincerely feel sorry. I hope you will forgive me as it was actually an inadvertent mistake. I assure and promise you that I will never let this happen again.

Yours sincerely,
Kunal Goswami

3. (i)

GIVE TILL IT HURTS!

Charity Drive for the Underprivileged Children

Date: Friday, 3rd August, 20XX

Time: 8 a.m. to 11 a.m.

Venue : The Assembly Area, St. Joseph's Convent School

All the students from classes 5th to 10th are requested to contribute to make the charity drive a success. Textbooks, notebooks, items of stationery and other things may be donated for the cause.

Be as generous as possible.

(ii) To principal@stxavierschool.org

Subject Invitation to Participate in a Donation Drive for Underprivileged Children

Respected Sir/Ma'am,

This is to inform you that our school, St. Joseph's Convent is conducting a 'Donation Drive' on Friday, 3rd August, 20XX for the underprivileged children living in the slum areas near our school. This event will be conducted from 8 a.m. to 11 a.m. in the Assembly Area of our school building.

We request you to motivate the students of your school to donate their used textbooks, unused notebooks, stationery, blazers, sweaters or shoes that are in good condition for this noble cause. Participation by students from your school will make a huge impact on the student community as a whole besides helping the slum children. Please help us make a difference!

We anticipate a positive response from you to make this drive a success. You are welcome to contact me for any further clarification.

Thanking you,

Your respectfully,
Aarti Sardana

Head Girl
St. Joseph's Convent School
Contact No. : 99885XXXXX

4. (i) (1) (b) getting rid of

(2) (a) moving suddenly to attack or capture

(ii) (c) Ingenuity

(iii) (a) Our attitude towards insects is one of fear and the thinking that they are creatures which do more harm than good so they are unnecessary.

(b) Man tries to exterminate insects because they contaminate food, carry diseases, devour crops and sting or bite without provocation.

(c) To prevent the ants from reaching the Aphids, the writer bound the base of the tree with sticky tape so that they did not dare to cross it; thus, making it impossible for the ants to reach the Aphids. However, it was not successful as the ants found another way to reach the Aphids and prove their intelligence.

(d) The writer says that knowing about insects does not make man change his attitude towards them because they spoil or eat our food and cause injuries to us by biting or stinging us.

(e) The leaves of the tree were beginning to wither in summer because clusters of tiny insects called Aphids were on the underside of the leaves.

(iv) The behaviour that we show towards insects is mostly one of fear and detestation. We often wage war on them for contaminating food, carrying diseases, devouring crops or stinging or biting us without provocation. But, we are also fascinated by them. We enjoy learning about them and can spend hours observing their actions and behaviour.

5. (i) (1) be given (2) suck (3) live (4) injecting

(5) coloured (6) fly (7) have (8) lies

(ii) (a) in (b) at (c) on (d) at

(e) until (f) after (g) across (h) during

(iii) (1) (b) My sister works three jobs in a day; however, she doesn't earn much money.

(2) (b) We went out despite the cold weather.

(3) (d) Though he was ill, he attended the meeting.

(4) (d) She is pretty as well as intelligent.

(iv) (1) (a) Every candidate should aim to pass the examination.

(2) (d) None of the above

(3) (b) No sooner did he get onto the bus than the driver started the engine.

(4) (b) He will not be pardoned unless he apologises.

(5) (a) A lot was eaten by the sheep.

(6) (d) Was this circle drawn by Sue?

(7) (c) Whenever there is effort, there is success.

(8) (b) He said that he was writing a letter.

SQP Code : **PB-3/10** Series ***i*-Succeed 3-25/10** Roll No.

Sample Question Paper 03

English Language 10th (Code 01)

General Instructions

1. You will not be allowed to write during the first 15 minutes. This time is to be spent in reading the question paper.
2. The time given at the head of this paper is the time allowed for writing the answers.
3. Attempt all five questions.
4. The intended marks for questions or parts of questions are given in brackets [].
5. You are advised to spend not more than 30 minutes in answering Question 1 and 20 minutes in answering Question 2.

Time : 2 Hrs.

Max. Marks : 80

Question 1.

(Do not spend more than 30 minutes on this question.)

Write a composition (300-350 words) on **any one** of the following. [20]

(i) Write an original short story entitled 'God helps those who help others.'

(ii) 'Online smart classes are the future of education.' Express your views for or against this statement.

(iii) Every year, the school holds a fair known as 'The Annual School Fete'. Describe what you see at the fete. Give details of the food, game and other stalls put up there.

(iv) You are a resident of London, England and are visiting India for the first time to attend a training course. Write an account of your experience and what you learnt on reaching there.

(v) Study the picture given below. Write a short story or a description or an account of what it suggests to you. Your composition may be about the subject of the picture or you may take suggestions from it; however, there must be a clear connection between the picture and your composition.

Question 2.

(Do not spend more than 20 minutes on it.)

Select **any one** of the following. [10]

(i) Write a letter to the Editor of a newspaper about the insanitary conditions prevailing in your locality and the indifference of the Municipal authorities in spite of repeated letters of complaint.

(ii) Your friend, Suraj, has cleared the prestigeous CAT examination. Write a letter congratulating him for his success expressing how proud you are of him.

Question 3.

(i) You are Manish/Mishita, the Secretary of Tours and Trips Society of Translam Academy International, Meerut. The school is organising a 20-day historical tour to some places inviting students interested in visiting those places. Write a notice in about 50 words to be put up on the school notice board. [5]

(ii) Write an email to your cousin Swinky with mail id swinky912@hotmail.com telling her about your recent 20-day historical tour. You are Kama. [5]

Question 4.

Read the following passage carefully and answer the questions that follow.

Apollo Hospital group has installed the world's most advanced Cyberknife robotic radio surgery system at the Cancer Speciality Centre in Chennai, India. Although it meant a substantial cost for the hospital, Apollo decided to go ahead with the project due to the new-found enthusiasm for robotics in India.

From the Chandrayaan-I project for sending robots to the Moon to biomedical engineering and the auto industry, India has been using robotics on a wide scale.

In an increasingly technology-driven country, robotics has fast assumed significance not only for industrial applications, but also for using in various day-to-day human activities. According to the Oxford Dictionary, robotics is the branch of technology that deals with the design, construction, operation, structural disposition, manufacture and application of robots.

The word robotics was derived from the word robot. It was first used in print by Isaac Asimov, in his science fiction story 'Liar!' published in May 1941, in the magazine Astounding Science Fiction. Today, it is a confluence of science using the continuing advancements of mechanical engineering, material science, sensor fabrication, manufacturing techniques and advanced algorithms.

Presently, robotics is at the **pinnacle** of technical development. Though robotics in India is at a nascent stage, industrial automation in India has opened up a huge potential for robotics. Innovation coupled with consolidated research and development has catapulted India's scientific position in robotic technology to a very high level. Analysts claim that the Indian manufacturing industry has been growing at an average rate of 10 percent to 12 percent per year and the global market for robots is projected to rise by an average of 4.2 percent, while in India, the industry is expected to grow at a rate 2.5 times that of the global average.

In medicine, the importance of robotics has been growing. Robotic surgery is a new and exciting emerging technology that holds significant promise. Robots are increasingly being used in a variety of clinical and surgical settings for increasing surgical accuracy and decreasing operating times. Often they create better healthcare outcomes than standard current approaches. Robotic technology will have a **tremendous** social and cultural impact on the future of healthcare. In providing healthcare, robots are expected to augment traditional treatment, resulting in humans and robots working side by side. It has been proven that robotic systems have benefited our society in many ways. For instance, some robots have helped children with developmental disabilities, others have improved the health status of people where as with different deficiencies. People who have experienced therapy robots in their lives have commented that robots brought confidence in their lives as well as solved problems related to health.

The other fact is that in some industrial countries robots are helping children with deficiencies to develop faster and have positively influenced their behaviour.

Experts predict that by 2020, robots will become more intelligent and irreplaceable as they would perform most household chores such as laundry and home maintenance. They would provide valuable services for children and elderly people. Thus, in the future, robots promise to play an important role in our lives.

(i) For each word given below, choose the correct meaning (as used in the passage) from the options provided. [2]

(1) *tremendous* (line 29)
(a) trivial (b) not able
(c) miniscule (d) infinitesimal

(2) *pinnacle* (line 17)
(a) nadir (b) trough (c) zenith (d) highest point

(ii) Which word in the passage means the opposite of the word 'surplus'? [1]
(a) augment (b) catapulted (c) deficiencies (d) disabilities

(iii) Answer the following questions briefly in your own words.
(a) In which sectors has India been using robotics? [2]
(b) What does 'robotics' mean? [2]
(c) Why are robots being increasingly used in clinical surgeries? [2]
(d) What is the current scientific position of India in robotic technology? [2]
(e) Which word or phrase in the passage denotes that setting up a radio surgery system was an expensive deal for Apollo Hospital group? [1]

(iv) Describe in your own words the present scenario of robotic technology in India and its growing influence in medicine. Do not exceed 50 words. [8]

Question 5.

(a) Fill in each of the numbered blanks with correct form of the words given in brackets. Do not copy the passage but write in correct serial order the word or phrase appropriate to the blank space. [8]

Example Ritika ....(0).........(talk) to her grandfather yesterday.

Answer : (0) talked

Single combat has been known to exist ever since man first ...**(1)**... (appear) on Earth. Early man had to ...**(2)**... (hunt) for his food and he ...**(3)**... (use) the same weapons in single combat as he did for ...**(4)**... (hunt). The development of weapons from the early clubs to the sword ...**(5)**... (vary) from country to country.

In the sixteenth century, fencing ...**(6)**... (bring) to England by the Italians. Junior fencers gained their qualifications by ...**(7)**... (fight) for a prize before their peers.

Fencing has since ...**(8)**... (become) a popular sport appealing to both men and women alike.

(ii) Fill in each blank with an appropriate words. [4]

(a) .... Peter and John, there were three other boys present.

(b) He was stabbed .... a lunatic with a dagger.

(c) She dislikes being looked ....

(d) Don't throw food .... the dog.

(e) I'm going for lunch and will be back .... 30 minutes.

(f) You have .... Thursday noon to submit your assignment.

(g) Michael Phelps won eight gold medals .... Beijing in 2008.

(h) I see a spider .... the door.

(iii) Join the following sentences to make one complete sentence **without using and, but** or **so**. Choose the correct option. [4]

(1) He is not educated. He possesses practical wisdom.
   (a) Though he is not educated but he possesses practical wisdom.
   (b) Though he is not educated yet he possesses practical wisdom.
   (c) Though he is not educated, he possesses practical wisdom.
   (d) None of the above

(2) They gave her the best treatment. They could not save her.
   (a) Although they gave her the best treatment, they could not save her.
   (b) Although they gave her the best treatment, yet they could not save her.
   (c) They gave her the best treatment in spite they could not save her.
   (d) None of the above

(3) God made small things. God made great things.
   (a) God made both small and great things.
   (b) God made small, great things.
   (c) Small things were made by God, so were great things.
   (d) God made small as well as great things.

(4) Martin is not tall. His father is also not tall.
   (a) Either Martin or his father is tall.
   (b) Either Martin or his father is not tall.
   (c) Neither Martin nor his father is not tall.
   (d) Neither Martin nor his father is tall.

(iv) Choose the correct option to rewrite the following according to instructions given after each sentence. [8]

(1) I saw Paul three years back. It's been a long time.
   [Rewrite using : for]
   (a) I haven't seen Paul for three years, long time.
   (b) I haven't seen Paul for a long time.
   (c) I have seen Paul for three years.
   (d) I have seen Paul for three years, which is a long time.

(2) It's not necessary to take a lot of luggage when going on holiday.
   [Use : much]
   (a) You needn't take much luggage when going on holiday.
   (b) You don't have to take much luggage when going on holiday.
   (c) You don't need much luggage when going on holiday.
   (d) All of the above

(3) Perhaps, he hasn't received the doctor's results yet.
[Use : may]
(a) You may not have received the doctor's results yet.
(b) He may not have received the doctor's results yet.
(c) He may have received the doctor's results yet.
(d) You may have received the doctor's results yet.

(4) The doorbell rang in the middle of her phone conversation.
[Rewrite using : while]
(a) The doorbell rang while she was speak on the phone.
(b) The doorbell was ringing while she was talking on the phone.
(c) The doorbell rang while she was talking on the phone.
(d) None of the above

(5) That letter arrived only a few minutes ago.
[Rewrite using : just]
(a) The letter arrived just.
(b) The letter has just arrived.
(c) Just the letter arrived.
(d) The letter has arrived just.

(6) Kerrie has paid the bill.
[Begin with : The bill...]
(a) The bill was paid by Kerrie.
(b) The bill has been paid by Kerrie.
(c) The bill had been paid by Kerrie.
(d) The bill is paid by Kerrie.

(7) Does the police officer catch the thief?
[Begin with : Is...]
(a) Is the thief being caught by the police officer?
(b) Is the thief being catch by the police officer?
(c) Is the thief catch by the police officer?
(d) Is the thief caught by the police officer?

(8) She said, 'I have finished the work.'
[Begin with : She said that...]
(a) She said that she finished the work.
(b) She said that she has finished the work.
(c) She said that she had finished the work.
(d) She said that the work was finished by her.

Answers *in Topper's Style*

1. (i)

God Helps those Who Help Others

Smriti got up late that day as her college was closed. Both her parents were working in different offices so they had left for the day. As she was preparing breakfast for herself, she suddenly remembered that she had promised to look after her sick uncle that day as her aunt had to visit a government office to get some work done. Smriti had promised her aunt that she would reach their home by 10 am so that her aunt could go for her work.

So, Smriti finished her breakfast quickly and was ready to go. Taking an auto-rickshaw, she went to her uncle's house. After her aunt left for work, Smriti sat and conversed with her uncle who was lying in bed. Then, she prepared a cup of ginger tea for him and brought it for him. As she started cooking *khichri* for his lunch, her phone rang. It was her mother who was yelling at her. Smriti could not understand what her mother was shouting about. The only thing she understood was that her mother was telling her to come home immediately.

Smriti left for home soon after cooking the *khichri* and giving it to her uncle. She had already made a call to her aunt and explained why she had to leave. On reaching home, to her horror, she was told by her mother, who had returned from office, that the house had been burgled. Apparently, in her hurry to reach her uncle's home, Smriti had left the front door unlocked. Thus, the burglar had an easy time stealing all their valuable items. The police were already there and were dusting various locations for fingerprints of the burglar.

The next day, they were pleasantly surprised to receive a phone call from the police station that informed them that the burglar had been caught due to his fingerprints. He had been in jail three times earlier for burglaries so the police knew where they could find him. The stolen valuables were also recovered from the burglar. Thus, Smriti realised that the saying 'God helps those who help others' is true.

(ii) **For the Motion**

Most parents currently think negatively about the effect of computers and smartphones on the children of school-going age. If such parents are so old-fashioned as to think that computers will be distracting children from their studies, then, with a very sincere apology to them, I wish to inform them that the young generation has come a long way with computers! Additionally, I want to make my audience aware of the endless possibilities of computer and internet-based teaching methods.

When most parents think of their children learning their lessons through online classes, social media websites such as Facebook appear before their eyes. Unfortunately, it is a tragedy that such parents are digitally uneducated. There is a large number of sites beyond Facebook. A number of websites and online platforms having the words 'Academy', 'Teaching App', 'Course', etc. in their names is on the World Wide Web and this number is increasing everyday.

There are millions of students and teachers who use these websites, apps and online platforms. Teachers use them for preparation of tests and exam papers while students use them for brushing up their concepts, practising their skills and preparing for exams. These online resources are mostly free as they make their money through advertisements and premium memberships which offer solutions to problems. This 'free' feature has turned students away from the traditional paper guides and coaching books available in the market. With a smartphone, tablet or laptop in almost every hand, in both urban and rural areas, these online sources are within everyone's reach. In fact, Google has replaced the original 'guru' to become the greatest knowledge-provider.

With the world's population increasing and the forest cover reducing, it is the need of the hour to go paperless. In this regard, we cannot find a better solution than e-learning. Rather than playing the role of a consumer, let us become contributors. Instead of using paper books, let us use e-books. Instead of collecting a thousand books on our shelves, let's use our phones, tablets and computers for attending online classes.

Against the Motion

Online learning or e-learning means learning conducted *via* electronic media, typically on the internet. Usually the online lessons, such as on YouTube, are prepared without having an accurate idea about the audience. Thus, if a particular lesson has been prepared keeping poor students in mind, teachers or good students may not find it useful. Conversely, if a lesson has been prepared for teachers, the poor students will not understand it at all. As there cannot be a face-to-face interaction between the 'online teacher' and the student before the lesson is prepared, there is no scope for adjusting and modifying the language or the concept accordingly. It can only be fine tuned after many users have given their feedback.

This may even take a few months, by which time the lesson may become useless for thousands of users who have accessed it. On the other hand, a teacher in a traditional classroom can modify the level and style of the lesson on the basis of instantaneous feedback received while it is being taught. In this way, the subject matter will be learnt more effectively. Moreover, human beings are known to be social animals. Thus, they are more interested in direct face-to-face interaction than interacting with a machine which does not reply immediately. In online mode, lessons lack proper guidance and self-assessment mechanisms.

Other activities in schools which help students to develop physically and mentally will not be possible to replicate online. For instance, as no real physical work is involved in online classes, students can get lethargic and also change physiologically. Next, they will not lead a disciplined life. Attending a traditional school makes one have a fixed time schedule so that one learns good habits such as punctuality in all activities, dressing in a uniform, eating proper meals, etc. Lastly, we should not forget the excellent interactions involved in physical learning. Children tend to make friends with those who support them and mentors who guide them. Thus, no matter how fast technological developments take place, the traditional way of learning should not be discarded.

(iii) **The Annual School Fete**

The school fete is an occasion looked forward to by all of us. In my school, it was held on 10th October this year. Feverish preparations began two weeks prior. Each class was asked to set up a stall of their choice. Contributions from the students were collected and invitations were sent to the parents, VIPs of the city and other prominent people.

The day arrived too soon and turned out to be cloudy. By mid-day, the Sun peeped through the clouds that hung heavy in the sky. The clouds threatened to ruin everything but thankfully a westerly breeze blew them steadily away, bringing much cheer to our dampened spirits.

It was exciting to see students manning the stalls, selling assorted items from raffle tickets to 'ring a gift', hoopla, target practice, etc. A giant wheel was running for small children who were shouting with delight as the wheel went round. There were also stalls of eatables selling snacks, chowmein, cakes, chocolates and cold beverages. There was even a tea stall for those who wanted to drink something warm.

The students were working as if they were true businessmen, accounting for cash and stocks. The stalls selling eatables were the most crowded. The occasional crackle of the loudspeaker broke the revelry to make an announcement.

A friendly tap on my shoulder made me turn around. "Hi, Mohit", said Devesh as he took my hand and escorted me to his stall selling raffle tickets. He persuaded me to buy one. I reluctantly parted with a ten rupee note in exchange for the ticket which I carelessly shoved in my back pocket. Thereafter, I had a gala time with my friends eating chowmein and ice cream till we had run out of money.

Just as I was about to depart, the microphone crackled to life to announce the number of the first prize winner in the lucky draw. I pulled out the crumbled ticket from my pocket. And lo and behold! I had struck the jackpot! In a trance, I walked up to the podium, to collect my prize which was a wonderful new tablet computer. I will never forget this day when I was introduced to the digital world in such a delightful manner.

(iv) My father passed away when I was 18 years old and left me enough money to complete my study of music, as I had got admission in a music academy for Indian classical arts in Mumbai. I was travelling to India for the first time. During those days, we had no direct flight from London to Mumbai. So, I had to change flights at Moscow.

Unfortunately, my connecting flight from Moscow to Mumbai was delayed because of a blizzard in Moscow. So, when I arrived in Mumbai, I was alone in a country I did not know much about. I decided to stay at a hotel for the night as it was late in the evening when I arrived. Next day, I went to the music academy I was to attend.

I arrived at the hotel in a taxi where people were asking for tips for everything: opening the door, bringing water for me, carrying my luggage, etc. When I saw my hotel room, I was shocked to find it in a shabby condition. The toilet was dirty and had a leaking tap. Thankfully, the shower was working! Although I was somewhat shocked at what I saw, I was infinitely more excited to see an Indian sunrise.

I woke up early the next morning and talked to the hotel staff about arranging a taxi to go to the music academy. The taxi driver confirmed that he knew where it was located. Little did I know that, in India, people almost never say 'no' even if they are not knowledgeable about anything. So, instead of the driver taking me to the music academy, he took me in another direction to an ashram of a spiritual teacher, or 'guru'.

But positivity can change one's outlook so I was not much concerned about getting lost. The people at the ashram helped me call the office of the music academy and so I was able to get the exact directions on how to reach there. Soon, I reached my destination and realised that a positive attitude can turn any bad experience into a joyful one.

(v) This given picture shows a part of the Wagah Border Ceremony, also called 'the Beating Retreat Ceremony', which is a daily military practice conducted at the border outpost of Wagah in Punjab. The security forces of both India and Pakistan take part in this exercise conducted at sunset every day. From the Indian side, soldiers of the Border Security Force (BSF) participate in this exercise. From the Pakistani side, the Pakistan Rangers carry out this exercise. The drill comprises elaborate and rapid colourful movements by soldiers of both sides. Thousands of people gather on either side of the border gates every evening to witness the ceremony. The event has many international viewers too.

Security guards man the borders on both sides. As the Sun sets, the iron gates at the border are opened and the two flags are lowered at the same time. The flags are folded and the ceremony ends with a retreat that involves a handshake between soldiers from either side, followed by the closing of the gates again. The ceremony is symbolic of the rivalry between the two nations. In addition, it is also a reflection of the goodwill and cooperation between India and Pakistan, two nations divided by politics but united by sentiments.

The Wagah border bears historical and political significance for people of both the countries and stands testimony to the Partition of 1947. It remains a cause for tension on the Indian subcontinent even today due to the mass killings that took place at that time. Some people are of the opinion that partition should have never happened. Others strongly favour partition and say that it was suitable for colonial India at that time. The ceremony at the Wagah border may be conducted by two nations but, in reality, the people on the Pakistan side are no different than the people on the Indian side. Citizens of both the nations still wish to cross the border without any fear or hatred and greet each other without any weapons and security.

2. (i)

102, Gumti No. 5,
Kanpur
4th April, 20XX

The Editor,
The Times of India,
Kanpur, Uttar Pradesh

Subject Insanitary conditions in Gokul Dham Colony

Dear Sir/Ma'am,

Through the column of your prestigious daily, I wish to draw the attention of the concerned authorities towards the extremely pitiable conditions in Gokul Dham Colony. Sanitation is the cornerstone of public health and our colony drastically lacks it. Improper disposal of domestic waste and open sewages have been causing catastrophic effects on the health of the children as well as the adults in our colony.

This, in turn, is giving rise to serious diseases like diarrhea, cholera, etc. Water-logging and open manholes are other sources of diseases like malaria. They have also posed a risk before parents who are scared of sending their children out for playing. Yet, the local authorities are indifferent to such a grave concern. This is not only astonishing but also shameful on their part.

I would like to request the civil authorities to show their concern in this regard and take necessary steps immediately.

Thanking you,

Yours sincerely,
Sima Kushwaha

(ii) 14/3 Ashok Vihar,
New Delhi

1st October, 20XX

Dear Suraj,

It was indeed a pleasure to hear from Dinesh that you have passed the CAT examination with 99 percentile and are expecting to get admission in one of the IIMs. Please accept my heartiest congratulations on this achievement. You really deserved it. Your hardwork and perseverance have paid you dividends. Your excellent result is owed to the immense hardwork and dedicated effort put in. Studying systematically and sacrificing your leisure has helped you crack the much dreaded CAT examination with flying colours!

I am sure both uncle and aunt are extremely proud of you. Please pay my sincere regards to them. However, the interview is a hard nut to crack too. Please prepare thoroughly well for it leaving no stone unturned.

Wishing you all the very best and hoping for complete success!

Tell me about your counselling and good luck for your interview. Congratulations!

Yours lovingly,
Ravi

3. (i)

Time for Tour!

20-day Tour to Historical Places
From 24th December, 20XX to 14th January, 20XX
for students of Classes IX – XII

Interested students must submit their parents' acceptance letter and deposit ₹ 2500 by 15th November, 20XX.

(ii) **To** swinky912@hotmail.com

Subject 20-day historical trip

Dear Swinky,

How are you? I am doing good here. It's been a long time and I desperately wanted to tell you about the 20-day tour organised by the Tours and Trips society of our school.

The trip organised was an amazing learning experience for us. We travelled across 7 states—Tamil Nadu, Kerala, Delhi, Assam, Maharashtra, Punjab and Gujarat. We visited various religious as well as historically important places like Rameshwaram Temple, Jallianwala Bagh, Kartavya Path, etc.

The glory of our past, our culture and our struggles to reach where our nation stands today were deeply imbibed in us throughout our trip.

There are many more things that I want to tell you and I will definitely tell you all about them when I visit you over the weekend. Till then, just imagine how fun the trip must have been.

Meeting you soon,
Yours lovingly
Kama

4. (i) (1) (b) notable (2) (d) highest point

(ii) (c) deficiencies

(iii) (a) India has been using robotics in the sectors of space exploration, biomedical engineering and the automobile industry. Recently, Apollo Hospital Group has installed world's most advanced Cyberknife robotic radio surgery system in a Cancer Speciality Centre in Chennai.

(b) 'Robotics' refers to the branch of technology that deals with the design, construction, operation, structural disposition, manufacture and application of robots.

(c) Robots are being increasingly used in clinical surgeries due to their higher surgical accuracy, reduced operating time and creation of better healthcare outcomes when compared with the currently standard approach to surgeries.

(d) The current scientific position of India in robotic technology is that it is at a very high level as Indian manufacturing industry has been growing at an average rate of 10% to 12% which is 2.5 times that of the global average.

(e) The phrase in the passage that denotes that it was an expensive deal is 'substantial cost' in the first paragraph.

(iv) The present scenario of robotic technology in India is bright due to its applications such as space exploration, automobile manufacture and medicine. In medicine, its use has increased for conducting surgical operations due its accuracy and speed. It can also create a more supportive environment for people with disabilities and deficiencies, installing confidence in their lives.

5. (i) (1) appeared (2) hunt (3) used (4) hunting
(5) varied (6) was brought (7) fighting (8) become

(ii) (a) Besides (b) by (c) at (d) to
(e) in (f) until (g) in (h) on

(iii) (1) (c) Though he is not educated, he possesses practical wisdom.
(2) (a) Although they gave her the best treatment, they could not save her.
(3) (d) God made small as well as great things.
(4) (d) Neither Martin nor his father is tall.

(iv) (1) (b) I haven't seen Paul for a long time.
(2) (d) All of the above
(3) (b) He may not have received the doctor's results yet.
(4) (c) The doorbell rang while she was talking on the phone.
(5) (b) The letter has just arrived.
(6) (b) The bill has been paid by Kerrie.
(7) (d) Is the thief caught by the police officer?
(8) (c) She said that she had finished the work.

SQP Code : **PB-4/15** Series ***i*-Succeed 4-25/10** Roll No.

Sample Question Paper 04

English Language 10th (Code 01)

General Instructions

1. You will not be allowed to write during the first 15 minutes. This time is to be spent in reading the question paper.
2. The time given at the head of this paper is the time allowed for writing the answers.
3. Attempt all five questions.
4. The intended marks for questions or parts of questions are given in brackets [].
5. You are advised to spend not more than 30 minutes in answering Question 1 and 20 minutes in answering Question 2.

Time : 2 Hrs.

Max. Marks : 80

Question 1.

(Do not spend more than 30 minutes on this question.)

Write a composition (300-350 words) on **any one** of the following. [20]

(i) Recall an important event of social importance in your city. Describe the event as it occurred and its impact on other members of the society.

(ii) 'Coaching classes are important for better learning.' Express your views *for* or *against* this statement.

(iii) Your school participated in 'Say No to Crackers' campaign organised by the municipality in your town one week before Diwali. Write an account of the activities undertaken during this campaign.

(iv) Write a short story beginning with the line: "It was a normal evening at the park. Children were playing on the rides, women were sitting and gossiping, two elderly gentlemen were sitting on the corner bench and sharing jokes. Every thing was the same as any other evening, except one thing. ...."

(v) Study the picture given below. Write a story or a description or an account of what the picture suggests to you. Your composition may be about the subject of the picture or you may take suggestions from it; however, there must be a clear connection between the picture and your composition.

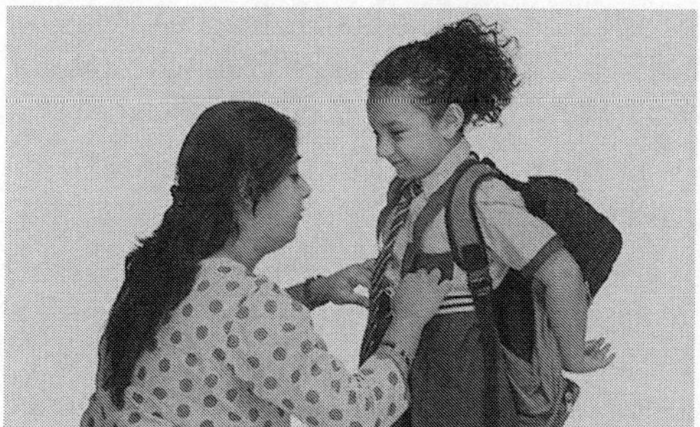

Question 2.

(Do not spend more than 20 minutes on this question)

Select **any one** of the following. [10]

(i) You had bought a mobile phone from a reputed showroom in Mumbai but, after a month, it developed a serious fault. Write a complaint letter to the Manager of the showroom asking for immediate replacement of the same. You are Sadiq/Razia, 123, South TT Nagar, Bhopal.

(ii) Write a letter to your cousin Rakesh congratulating him on getting an overseas job that he wanted to get. You are Rajendra.

Question 3.

(i) Write a notice for a meeting of security employees to discuss security hazards and arrive at a specific resolution to ensure maximum security for the school event. Give the agenda of the meeting in the notice. [5]

(ii) Write an email to the Principal of your school informing him/her about the event that you have planned and inviting her/him to judge the competition. [5]

Question 4.

Read the following story carefully and answer the questions that follows.

The Lord was the creator of good teachers. It was his sixth day of 'overtime' and he knew that this was a tremendous responsibility, for teachers would touch the lives of so many impressionable young children. An Angel appeared to him and said, "You are taking a long time to figure this one out." "Yes," said the Lord, "but have you read the specifications on this order?"

TEACHER: Teacher must stand above all students to be at their level. He must be able to do 180 additional things which are not related to their taught subject. Teacher must have to run on coffee. He must be able to communicate as per his vital knowledge to all students daily. Teacher must have more time for others than for himself, besides being supportive.

"Six pairs of hands, "said the Angel, "that's impossible"

"Well," said the Lord, "it is not the hands that are the problem. It is the three pairs of eyes that are presenting the most difficulty!"

The Angel looked incredulous, "Three pairs of eyes...on a standard model?"

The Lord nodded his head, "One pair is to see whether a student is doing or not what others have labelled them. The second pair is the pair of eyes which is at the back of the teacher's head to watch what should not be seen, but what must be known. The third pair is the eyes in the front which is only to look at the child and 'act out' in order to **reflect**, "I understand and I still believe in you", without so much as saying a word to the child."

"Lord," said the Angel, "this is a very large project and I think you should work on it tomorrow."

"I can't," said the Lord, "for I have come very close to creating something much like myself. I have one that comes to work when he/she is sick, teaches a class of children that do not want to learn, has a special place in his/her heart for children who are not his/her own, understands the struggles of those who have difficulty and never takes the students for granted."

The Angel looked closely at the model the Lord was creating.
"It is too soft-hearted," said the Angel.

"Yes,"said the Lord, "but also tough, you cannot imagine what this teacher can endure or do, if necessary." "Can this teacher think?" asked the Angel.
"Not only think," said the Lord, "but reason and compromise." The Angel came closer to have a better look at the model and ran his finger over the teacher's cheek.

"Well, Lord," said the Angel, Your job looks fine but there is a leak. I told you that you were putting too much into this model. You cannot imagine the stress that will be placed upon the teacher." The Lord moved in closer and lifted the drop of moisture from the teacher's cheek. It shone and glistened in the light.

"It is not a leak," He said, "It is a tear."

"A tear? What is that?" asked the Angel, "What is a tear for?" The Lord replied with great thought, "For the joy and pride of watching what a child accomplishes even it's the smallest task to do. It is done for the loneliness of children who have a hard time to fit into the compassionate feelings of their parents. This has been done when a teacher had to leave the class and to say good bye to his students and get ready to welcome a new class."

"My, "said the Angel," The tear thing is a great idea...You are a genius!"

The Lord looked sombre, "I didn't put it there."

(i) For each word given below, choose the correct meaning (as used in the passage) from the options provided. [2]

(1) *supportive* (line 9)
(a) to be encouraging
(b) to be sympathetic
(c) to be helpful
(d) All of these

(2) *reflect* (line 17)
(a) absorb
(b) think deeply or carefully
(c) let something be forgotten
(d) not take into consideration

(ii) Which word in the passage means the opposite of the word 'disagreement'? [1]
(a) compromise (b) reason (c) compassionate (d) sombre

(iii) Answer the following questions briefly in your own words.
(a) When did God create teachers? Why is this creation a tremendous responsibility? [2]
(b) What are the specifications for a teacher? [2]
(c) What is the teacher's tear for? [2]
(d) What is presenting the most difficulty to God? Why does a teacher need three pairs of eyes? [2]
(e) What are special qualities of a teacher according to God? [1]

(iv) In not more than 50 words, describe how did God envision 'creating a good teacher'. [8]

Question 5.

(i) Fill in each of the numbered blanks with the correct form of word given in brackets. Do not copy the passage but write in correct serial order the word or phrase appropriate to the blank space. [4]

Example There **...(0)...** (be) some confusion in the hall when I entered there.
Answer (0) was

The car ......**(1)**...... (slow) down at the curve. There ...... **(2)**......(be) a large crowd at the place. I......**(3)**...... (get) down from the car to see what ......**(4)** ...... (happen). A man was ...... **(5)** ...... (lay) on the road injured. He ...... **(6)** ...... (shout) for help but ...... **(7)** ......(unfortunate) no one was willing to ...... **(8)** ......(come) forward and rush him to the hospital.

(ii) Fill in the blanks with appropriate words. [4]
(a) The people are sitting .... the table .... the dining room.
(b) The stairs to the roof are .... the bathroom .... the second floor.
(c) The children's bedroom is .... the attic .... the third floor.
(d) The washing machine is .... the main bathroom.

(e) The steps are in .... of the drawing room door.
(f) The tools are hung .... the wooden nail board.
(g) The wooden nail board is .... the basement.
(h) The basement is .... the drawing room of the house.

(iii) Join the following sentences to make one complete sentence **without using and, but** or **so.** Choose the correct option. [4]

(1) Saroja was a skilled Kathak dancer. Her mother wanted her to become a doctor.
(a) Her mother wanted her to become a doctor yet Saroja was a skilled Kathak dancer.
(b) Although Saroja was a skilled Kathak dancer, her mother wanted her to become a doctor.
(c) Since Saroja was a skilled Kathak dancer, her mother wanted her to become a doctor.
(d) Her mother wanted her to a doctor despite Saroja was a skilled Kathak dancer.

(2) Salim was thrown out of the community hall by the priest. His family protested outside the priest's house.
(a) Because Salim was thrown out of the community hall by the priest, his family protested outside the priest's house.
(b) Although Salim was thrown out of the community hall by the priest, his family protested outside the priest's house.
(c) Whenever Salim was thrown out of the community hall by the priest, his family protested outside the priest's house.
(d) While Salim was thrown out of the community hall by the priest, his family protested outside the priest's house.

(3) Mihir worked day and night on his project. The supervisor selected Jagdish's project for the exhibition.
(a) Though Mihir worked day and night on his project yet the supervisor selected Jagdish's project for the exhibition.
(b) Although Mihir worked day and night on his project, but the supervisor selected Jagdish's project for the exhibition.
(c) Though Mihir worked day and night on his project, the supervisor selected Jagdish's project for the exhibition.
(d) None of the above

(4) I went to the clinic yesterday. I met my former colleague Ravinder there.
(a) Since I went to the clinic yesterday, I met my former colleague Ravinder there.
(b) Whenever I went to the clinic yesterday, I met my former colleague Ravinder there.
(c) When I went to the clinic yesterday, I met my former colleague Ravinder there.
(d) As I went to the clinic yesterday, I met my former colleague Ravinder there.

(iv) Choose the correct option to rewrite the following according to the instructions given after each sentence. [8]

(1) He really likes correcting her English.
[Use : pleasure]
(a) He really likes pleasure in correcting her English.
(b) There is pleasure for him correcting English.
(c) He takes pleasure to correct her English.
(d) He takes pleasure in correcting her English.

(2) I didn't hear from him for ten years. I received his e-mail.
[Rewrite using: when]
(a) I hadn't heard from him for ten years when I received his e-mail.
(b) I haven't heard from him for ten years when I received his e-mail.
(c) I didn't heard for him for ten years when I received his e-mail.
(d) I didn't heard from him for ten years when I received his e-mail.

(3) She started studying drama three years ago.
[Rewrite using : been]
(a) She was been studying drama for three years.
(b) She was been studied drama for three years.
(c) She has been studying drama for three years.
(d) All of the above

(4) All I want you to do is to look after my dog.
[Use : care]
(a) All I want you to do is to look care of my dog.
(b) All I want you to do is to take care of my dog.
(c) All I want you to do is care of my dog.
(d) None of the above

(5) A father is wrong to scold his child without reason.
[Begin with: A father ought......]
(a) A father ought to scold his child without reason.
(b) A father ought not to scold her child without reason.
(c) A father ought not to scold his child without reasoning.
(d) A father ought not to scold his child without reason.

(6) He locked the gate so that the dog wouldn't escape.
[Use : prevent]
(a) He locked the gate for prevent the dog from escaping.
(b) He locked the gate for prevent the dog from not escaping.
(c) He locked the gate to prevent the dog from not escaping.
(d) He locked the gate to prevent the dog from escaping.

(7) They did not like to pay extra taxes.
[Use : objected]
(a) They did not objected to paying extra taxes.
(b) They objected to paying extra taxes.
(c) They did object to paying extra taxes.
(d) They did objected to paying extra taxes.

(8) The day was so nice that we went on a picnic.
[Use : such]
(a) It was such a nice day that we went on a picnic.
(b) It was such a nice day than we went on a picnic.
(c) The day was such nice that we went on a picnic.
(d) The day was such nice than we went on a picnic.

Answers in Topper's Style

1. (i) A mega blood donation camp was organised on the 1st of July in my city as well as in other cities. It was organised by the youth wing of the Lions Club. I was determined to be a part of this camp. This time, youth wing was going to organise blood donation camps in every city and town all over India and make it to the Guinness World Record. The advertisements about blood donation camp were given in newspapers, television and social media. The purpose was to create awareness and rage amongst the public. Facebook was flooded with likes and comments. Messages were also exchanged on WhatsApp.

My father was a member of the Lions Club and incharge of the committee which was formed to organise the camp in our city. Groups of youth were formed who went door-to-door to convince people about the importance of blood donation. There were a lot of myths in the minds of the general public. The children's wing organised a poster regarding these myths. The posters were put up at different places like shopping malls, movie halls, shopping stores for people to see and learn the benefits of donating blood.

When the final day arrived, I reached the venue quite early. The chief guest for the occasion was the District Magistrate of our city. Other people present included the local MLA and the councillors of city. The event was announced open by cutting a ribbon by the chief guest. The beds were placed in a hall at the Lions Club. A team of doctors and technicians along with their equipments were ready. People in large numbers had lined up for donating blood. The person was taken to a bed and 300 units of bloods were taken from each healthy person. By the end of the day, around 5 pm, six hundred and forty seven people had donated their blood. Figures from all over India were also coming on WhatsApp. This event turned out to be a huge success and people were quite enthusiastic to donate blood and be part of this camp. It was organised with enthusiasm and we were happy that it was put on record by the Guinness World Record. The Chief Guest congratulated everyone and promised to continue with such events in future too.

(ii) **For the Motion**

Coaching institutes provide better guidance as to what and how syllabus needs to be prepared for senior classes so that students are able to shape themselves accordingly for competitive exams, entrance exams, etc. In coaching institutes, the students not only get the correct academic guidance but they are also able to identify and learn about more career options and choose the right path as per their interest and academic record. They are really helpful regarding where you can start your career and seek good career guidance.

In school, teachers have to deal with 40-50 students in the class so they just focus on covering their syllabus in the time allotted to them. At coaching institutes, each student gets individual attention for all the subjects that they show interest for.

Coaching institutes develop different learning techniques according to every student which helps them in understanding their subjects well. In contrast, in school, all students of the same class get to learn the concepts in the same pattern. In coaching institutes, the learning pattern can be developed after an analysis of how a student adapts the concepts. When a student gets to learn in their own way, their understanding and grip on the subject develops quickly and, hence, they show improved results.

In school, if due to some reason a student is absent, he/she misses out on the important topics and loses track of their studies. Students are not able to cover the missed-concepts even if they want to because every day they have to follow the ongoing concepts in the classroom. But, in the coaching institutes, they get to learn topics as per their comfort and cover each concept that they miss out at school. In school, students fail to understand comprehensive concepts whereas the same they learn with ease in coaching institutes and, even if they fail to understands it in one attempt, they can ask the same thing multiple times for clarity. Thus, coaching classes surely help students understand a concept in a better manner.

Against the Motion

It should be emphasised that students today are undergoing immense stress due to their strong ambitions and the cut-throat competition between then for higher marks. The immense pressure on the students due to these two factors forces them to go for coaching classes. As the students are not able to get individual attention or get their doubts cleared in school, they enrol in coaching classes solely for this purpose. Further, their parents willingly bear the extra expense of coaching as they want their children to do well in school.

Coaching classes take up all the students' free time so they don't get to play any games or relax for sometime. However, even in coaching classes, students do not get enough individual attention because the number of students attending has grown beyond capacity.

The students are made to continuously practice answering the questions without the answers being properly checked or feedback given to the students about where they went wrong. This feedback is crucial for students to improve their responses to the questions. Thus, the majority of coaching classes cannot be termed as necessary for better learning.

On the other hand, the culture of coaching is eating into parents' pockets as such organisations charge very high fees although they may be coaching a student for only two hours per day. Further, both the parents and students rely heavily on these coaching classes as they have very high reputation but do not show results which match their reputations.

That is why learning at schools should be made so comprehensive that there is no need for any extra coaching. Also, regular doubt clearing sessions should be held in schools to enable students to understand the concepts better. There is an urgent need to overhaul the education system to make it stress-free so that coaching institutions are not required at all.

(iii)

'Say No to Crackers' Campaign

by Kavita Shah

Our school students participated as volunteers in the anti-crackers campaign organised by the Municipal Corporation one week before Diwali. Students from our school's secondary and senior secondary sections who volunteered were asked to report at 10 a.m. on the first day at the Town Hall. The town Mayor and councillors, along with some municipal officials, were present.

The Mayor started the meeting by announcing that the campaign would be called 'Say No to Crackers'. It would continue right up to the day of Diwali. He told the students that their duty would be to go from house to house in the localities where they lived and make the residents aware of the harmful effects of exploding crackers. They were asked to repeat a pledge spoken by the Mayor to not burn any cracker during the Diwali celebrations.

Then, a municipal official conducted a presentation on the various harmful effects of exploding crackers. These effects included air pollution due to the chemicals released, noise pollution due to the loud sounds, disturbance to the elderly, students preparing for exams, sleeping infants and so on.

Pamphlets highlighting these issues had been printed in bulk. One bundle of such pamphlets was handed over to each student for distribution in each home. The meeting concluded with the Mayor asking all the participants to meet in the Town Hall on the day after Diwali to provide feedback on the results of the campaign.

All the volunteers went round their localities with enthusiasm to distribute the pamphlets and educate the people about celebrating a quiet Diwali. In most homes, they were received with assurances that crackers would not be exploded. Most of these assurances came true as, even on the day of Diwali, the noise was much less than earlier years. Thus, most of the people of our town did actually 'say no to crackers'.

On the day after Diwali, at the Town Hall, the Mayor congratulated the student volunteers on the success of the campaign. He urged them to join the campaign next year too. The meeting ended with a grand party which the students thoroughly enjoyed.

(iv) It was a normal evening at the park. Children were playing on the rides, women were sitting and gossiping, two elderly gentlemen were sitting on the corner bench and sharing jokes. Every thing was the same as any other evening, except one thing. Sharmila was missing today. Sharmila was a 15-year-old girl who had lost her left leg in a car accident a few months ago. As the leg was crushed till above the knee by a truck which hit the car she was travelling in, the leg had to be amputated.

Sharmila was confined to a wheelchair but continued her studies in the school in which she had been studying before the accident. In the evenings, she used to visit the park in her wheelchair along with her mother. But today, she and her mother were missing. As it was highly unusual for Sharmila to miss an evening at the park, some of the children decided to find out what had happened to her. So, they went to her home.

There, they met Sharmila's younger brother who was alone at home. He informed them that Sharmila had gone with their parents to the Artificial Limbs Manufacturing Centre near Kanpur, about 80 kms away, for getting fitted with an artificial leg so that she would no longer be confined to a wheelchair. Her brother also informed them that Sharmila would be reaching home any moment now. Then, they heard the sound of a horn near the front door. Sharmila had arrived!

The children quickly opened the door and jumped with joy to see Sharmila walking slowly towards them without a crutch. Although she was limping, she embraced them one by one. Then, she happily told them that it was only a matter of a few days before she adjusted herself to walking with the artificial leg. Then, she would walk normally without any sign of her disability. She told the children that, after some practice, she would be also able to run although not at the same speed as before the accident. The children were overjoyed that Sharmila would be able to play with them as before.

(v) As the picture suggests, a small girl is getting ready to go to school. Her mother is busy in dressing her up. This is a normal routine at so many households where school going children are sent to school and major help to prepare them comes from children's mother. Elementary education is a Fundamental Right for India's children according to the Right to Education Act. Parents should ensure that their daughters get education as they deserve it. The family should not involve them so much in domestic duties that they neglect their schooling. It is famously said- "If you educate a man, you educate an individual; but, if you educate a woman, you educate the entire nation."

If the number of well-educated women in our country equals the number of men, these women will become capable of bringing about fundamental socio-economic changes in the Indian society. Their education will lead to their empowerment which will ultimately make the country prosperous. When girls in Indian society are educated, our society's sustainability and growth is ensured. However, if they remain uneducated and economically dependent on men, they will be helpless. Their economic independence can only come once they get educated and thus become suitable for employment.

Poverty is one of the major problems still existing in India and women education is a prerequisite to alleviate poverty. This would demand a big contribution from the educated women as they will have to motivate the uneducated girls and women to complete their education. An educated and progressive mother, wife, sister or daughter will help to educate the future generation of India. It will lead to a more enlightened and aware population which will fulfill the potential of India's demographic dividend and lead to prosperity for the nation.

2. (i) 123, South TT Nagar,
Bhopal- 462003

17th November, 20XX

The Manager,
Multimedia Stores,
345/7, Dr Bhadkarmkar Marg,
Mumbai - 400004

Subject Complaint regarding a faulty phone

Dear Sir/Ma'am,
On my last visit to Mumbai, I had bought an Apple iPhone7 Sr No. 7778906 from your showroom on 16th October, 20XX. The cash memo number is MS/456/17-18. Unfortunately, the phone stopped working yesterday which is very surprising for such a high quality product. It has not been damaged in any way by me.
So, you are requested to take action for free replacement of this phone as the phone is under warranty period. You are welcome to contact me on mobile no. 98765XXXXX for any clarification.

Thanking you,

Yours faithfully,
Sadiq

(ii) H No 506, Gopal Bari,
Kolkata

10th July, 20XX

Dear Rakesh,
I am delighted to hear from your sister that you have been offered the overseas job in the field and in the company that you had wanted to get.
You really worked very hard. You indeed deserved it. This is the result of your dedication, devotion and hard work. I am really proud of your success. I hope you will keep it up in future also.

What are your plans now? Write to me soon.
Convey my regards to your parents.

Yours lovingly,
Rajendra

3. (i) **Security Staff Meeting**

Date: Wednesday, 23rd February, 20XX

Time: 9 a.m. onwards

Venue: Room 121 XYZ, School

The purpose of the meeting is to discuss
- hazards faced recently
- suggestions for improving safety measures
- schedule for practice drills and training

All security guards and supervisors are required to attend the meeting to ensure that the upcoming school event is organised without any problems.

(ii) **To** Principalxyz@gmail.com

Subject Invitation to the upcoming Inter-House Dance Competition

Respected Sir/Ma'am,
This is to inform you that we, the students of Class IX to XII, have organised a dance competition with the help of our teacher as a part of inter house activity. The event will take place on 15th May, 20XX from 12:00 pm onwards in the school auditorium. We would be honored to have you as our chief guest and judge, and look forward to seeing you at the event.

We hope for a positive reply.

Thanking you,

Yours sincerely,

XYZ

4. (i) (1) (d) All of these (2) (b) think deeply or carefully

(ii) (a) compromise

(iii) (a) God created teachers on the sixth day of his 'overtime'.

This creation is a tremendous responsibility because teachers touch the lives of many impressionable children.

(b) The specifications for a teacher are

- He/she must stand above all students to be at their level.
- He/she must be able to communicate as per his/her vital knowledge to all students daily.
- He/she must have more time for others than for himself/herself.

(c) The teacher's tear is for the joy and pride of watching what a child accomplishes even if it's the smallest task to do. It is shed for the loneliness of children who have a hard time to fit into the compassionate feelings of their parents. This has been done when a teacher had to leave the class and to say good bye to his students and get ready to welcome a new class.

(d) Making the three pairs of eyes is presenting the most difficulty to God. A teacher needs three pairs of eyes because one pair is to see whether a student is doing or not what others have labelled them. The second pair which is at the back of the teacher's head is to watch what should not be seen but what must be known. The third pair is the eyes in the front which is only to look at the child and 'act out' in order to reflect 'I understand and I still believe in you' without saying a word to the child.

(e) According to God, a teacher's special qualities consist of being soft-hearted and caring as well as very tough when it comes to disciplining the child. Also, the teacher is able to think, reason well and can be very understanding and compromising. He/she is a blend of soft-heartedness and toughness.

(iv) According to God's vision, a good teacher must have additional pair of hands and eyes to carry out additional things besides teaching the students. An ideal teacher will be very committed to his/her work motivating the unwilling learners and treating his/her class children well. He/she should understand the problems of children from their perspectives and find out a solution to each problem.

5. (i) (1) slowed (2) was (3) got (4) had happened

(5) lying (6) was shouting (7) unfortunately (8) come

(ii) (a) at, in (b) beside, on (c) under, on (d) in

(e) front (f) on (g) in (h) under/below/beneath

(iii) (1) (b) Although Saroja was a skilled Kathak dancer, her mother wanted her to become a doctor.

(2) (a) Because Salim was thrown out of the community hall by the priest, his family protested outside the priest's house.

(3) (c) Though Mihir worked day and night on his project, the supervisor selected Jagdish's project for the exhibition.

(4) (c) When I went to the clinic yesterday, I met my former colleague Ravinder there.

(iv) (1) (d) He takes pleasure in correcting her English.

(2) (a) I hadn't heard from him for ten years when I received his e-mail.

(3) (c) She has been studying drama for three years.

(4) (b) All I want you to do is to take care of my dog.

(5) (d) A father ought not to scold his child without reason.

(6) (d) He locked the gate to prevent the dog from escaping.

(7) (b) They objected to paying extra taxes.

(8) (a) It was such a nice day that we went on a picnic.

SQP Code : **PB-5/10** Series ***i*-Succeed 5-25/10** Roll No. | | | | | | | | |

Sample Question Paper 05

English Language 10th (Code 01)

General Instructions

1. You will not be allowed to write during the first 15 minutes. This time is to be spent in reading the question paper.
2. The time given at the head of this paper is the time allowed for writing the answers.
3. Attempt all five questions.
4. The intended marks for questions or parts of questions are given in brackets [].
5. You are advised to spend not more than 30 minutes in answering Question 1 and 20 minutes in answering Question 2.

Time : 2 Hrs.

Max. Marks : 80

Question 1.

(Do not spend more than 30 minutes on this question.)

Write a composition (300-350 words) on **any one** of the following. [20]

(i) Write an original short story with a happy ending titled 'The Lazy Donkey'.

(ii) 'Social networking has a bad effect on teenagers.'
Express your views for or against this statement.

(iii) After attending a birthday party, you were picked up by your mother in her car. Suddenly, your mother's car was hit by a speeding vehicle and both you and your mother got injured. Write an account of your experience and the accident.

(iv) You have returned to your city Delhi after spending five years in a foreign country; the city has changed during your absence. Describe the changes that have affected people's life in the city. Give your views regarding these changes.

(v) Study the picture given below. Write a story or a description or an account of what it suggests to you. Your composition may be about the subject of the picture or you may take suggestions from it; however, there must be a clear connection between the picture and your composition.

Question 2.

(Do not spend more than 20 minutes on this question.)

Select **any one** of the following. [10]

(i) You are Sudhir/Sita, the Head Boy/Girl of ABC Public School, Jayanagar, Bengaluru. Your school has planned an overnight excursion of students and teachers to Mysuru and nearby areas. Write a letter to the Secretary, Ace Youth Hostel, Mysuru requesting him to send you a quotation for the costs of providing accommodation for 15 girls, 20 boys and 2 teachers for 2 days next month. Specify the dates when you want the accommodation and any other terms and conditions.

(ii) Write a letter to your friend, Shrawan consoling him on the death of his mother. Assume yourself to be Kushal.

Question 3.

(i) You are Abhishek/Avantika of Class XII, Swami Vivekanand Public School. Being an Activity Coordinator, draft a notice to all the other Activity Council members to discuss and plan the activities for 25th December (Christmas Day) celebrations. [5]

(ii) Write an e-mail to the Principal of a neighbouring school requesting him/her to send a team of teachers to judge an event organised for the 25th December Christmas Day celebrations. [5]

Question 4.

Read the following passage carefully and answer the questions that follow.

Lucie, a student from the United States, has just arrived at Charles de Gaulle in Paris, the airport that greets a million visitors to Paris every day. Paris, finally. It's always been a dream of Lucie to live in the city of light, the city of fine arts, of the Latin Quarter, of wine and, who knows, the city of a little love story perhaps. She plans to study in France for one year, to get her degree in Computer Science at the University of Versailles St. Quentin-en-Yvelines. It's the university that offered her a **scholarship** to study. Plus, her friend Josephine studies there so that Lucie can live with her in a small apartment.

She takes the RER train which brings her straight to the St Lazare Station at the city center. After arriving there, she looks for Versailles. She boards the train and soon it's heading into a black tunnel towards Versailles. Lucie is a little **disappointed** because she has to stay in Versailles when she'd like to live in Paris. But, she tells herself that Versailles is only a few minutes by train from the big city of Paris and, moreover, there are several attractions in Versailles.

The train exits the tunnel and, while passing the big city, she sees a large cemetery, the Eiffel Tower and Montmartre with the Sacre Coeur Cathedral nearby. A few moments later she arrives at the Versailles Station.

She has arrived. This is her destination. In front of her is the grand Chateau of Versailles where Lucie 14th, the Sun king, had parties and lived the high life with his mistresses. To the right is the avenue St. Cloud where the apartment that she'll live in with Josephine is located. She is tired but joyful. She starts looking for the address of the apartment. "All alone in a new country, knowing no one, future I'm ready!" Lucie says to herself. Lucie has arrived at the Versailles train station.

She has already seen the Chateau of Versailles but she wants to come back later for a more in-depth visit. But, she walks along avenue St. Loud first to find her apartment. She finds the address in front of the police station in a little brick house. She sets her bags down in front of the gate of the little pathway that leads to the sidewalk of the house. She rings the yellow doorbell next to 'Josephine Gerard'. Her friend, Josephine, whom she met on the web, opens the door. Josephine gives her two kisses. Shocked Lucie asks why she did that. That's how it's done in France.

SP-05

Girls give each other two kisses, guys give two kisses to girls and guys shake each other's hands. We do all this to say hello, Josephine says 'Come with me', says Josephine. "I'll show you the apartment. It's small but it's our own little place." Silently, Lucie follows her. Awed, she looks at the apartment's entryway. She can't believe her eyes when she enters the hallway and sees the walls are painted red, completely red. The floors are wood, beautiful and possible oak. The ceiling is painted black.

On the left is an iron table with the telephone on it. She goes on and to the left is a bathroom which is across from Josephine's room. A little farther, to the right, is Lucie's room. She puts all of her things in the corner, jumps into the bed and stretches her arms and legs. "Finally at my own place", she says to herself.

(i) For each word given below, choose the correct meaning (as used in the passage) from the options provided. [2]

(1) *scholarship* (line 6)
(a) grant to support a student's education
(b) tuition fees
(c) application to support a student's education
(d) procedure for studying abroad

(2) *disappointed* (line 10)
(a) pleased
(b) reluctant
(c) angry
(d) displeased as her hopes have not been fulfilled

(ii) Which word in the passage means the opposite of the word 'source'? [1]
(a) tunnel (b) destination (c) cemetery (d) apartment

(iii) Answer the following questions briefly in your own words.
(a) What are the two reasons for Lucie to take admission to the University of Versailles? [2]
(b) How does Lucie console herself about living in Versailles? What is her sorrow? [2]
(c) Why does Lucie say, 'Finally, at my own place' according to you? [2]
(d) How do people say, 'hello' in France? [2]
(e) What is Lucie ready for? [1]

(iv) Describe the apartment in which Lucie goes to stay, right from the entry in your own words. Do not exceed 50 words. [8]

SP-05

Question 5.

(i) Fill in each of the numbered blanks with correct form of the words given in brackets. Do not copy the passage but write in correct serial order the word or phrase appropriate to the blank space. [4]

Example

Coffee is a beverage ......**(0)**...... (drink) by many past generations of people.

Answer (0) drunk

What most people do not realise is that coffee is ......**(1)**...... (make) from beans ......**(2)**...... (pick) from trees.

Coffee trees ......**(3)**...... (grow) either from seeds or cuttings. These trees will begin to ......**(4)**...... (bear) crops when they are about four years old.

Workers on coffee plantations have to pick the beans by hand. After the beans ......**(5)**...... (gather), they are ......**(6)**...... (roast) at high temperatures. This process ......**(7)**......(give) them their fragrance.

The best coffee is made from freshly ......**(8)**...... (grind) beans. There are many different ways of preparing coffee. Coffee can be served either with or without milk.

(ii) Fill in each blank with an appropriate word. [4]

(a) I slept ...... nine o'clock.

(b) I commenced work ...... 1st May.

(c) We walked ...... the end of the street.

(d) The child has been missing ...... yesterday.

(e) He travelled seventy miles ...... two hours.

(f) I received this message ...... 7 o'clock in the morning.

(g) I saw him felling a big tree ......a hatchet.

(h) An old feud existed ...... the two families.

(iii) Join the following sentences to make one complete sentence **without using and, but** or **so**. Choose the correct option. [4]

(1) Alice seems to be quite intelligent. She often gets poor grades.
(a) Alice seems to be quite intelligent; otherwise, she often gets poor grades.
(b) Alice seems quite intelligent; therefore, she often gets poor grades.
(c) Alice seems quite intelligent; nonetheless, she often gets poor grades.
(d) Though Alice seems quite intelligent, but she often gets poor grades.

(2) This restaurant has some of the best chefs in the town. Their service is excellent.
(a) This restaurant has some of the best chefs in the town; moreover, their service is excellent.
(b) This restaurant has some of the best chefs in the town; however, their service is excellent.
(c) Even if this restaurant has some of the best chefs in the town, their service is excellent.
(d) This restaurant has some of the best chefs in the town because their service is excellent.

(3) I've never been to the US. I have friends and relatives there.
(a) I've never been to the US despite of having friends and relatives there.
(b) I've never been to the US while I have friends and relatives there.
(c) I've never been to the US in spite of having friends and relatives there.
(d) I've never been to the US after having friends and relatives there.

(4) He is a reckless driver. He hasn't had any accidents.
(a) Even though he is a reckless driver, yet he hasn't had any accidents.
(b) Though he is a reckless driver, he hasn't had any accidents.
(c) He is a reckless driver; moreover, he hasn't had any accidents.
(d) He is a reckless driver; therefore, he hasn't had any accidents.

(iv) Choose the correct option to rewrite the following according to instructions given after each sentence. [8]

(1) This horse is better trained than yours.
[Begin : Your........]
(a) Your horse is not as well trained as that.
(b) Your horse is not as well trained as this.
(c) Your is not as well trained as this horse.
(d) Your horse is not well trained as that horse.

(2) The children will sit out in the garden if the weather is cool.
[Begin : The children won't................]
(a) The children won't sit out in the garden if the weather is cool.
(b) The children won't be sitting out in the garden unless the weather was hot.
(c) The children won't sit out in the garden if the weather is hot.
(d) None of the above

(3) The thief ran so fast that the police could not catch him.
[Rewrite using : too]
(a) The thief ran too fast that he could not be caught.
(b) The thief ran fast that the police couldn't catch him.

(c) The thief ran too fast to be caught by the police.
(d) The thief ran too fast to have the police catch him.

(4) Her attitude often annoys me.
[Rewrite using : annoyance]
(a) Her attitude often leads her to annoyance.
(b) Annoyance is often caused to her.
(c) Annoyance is the effect of her attitude.
(d) Her attitude is often the cause of my annoyance.

(5) It was unkind of you to talk to her like that.
[Use : not]
(a) It was unkind of you to not talk to her like that.
(b) You should not have not talked to her like that.
(c) You should not have talked to her like that.
(d) It was not unkind of you to talk to her like that.

(6) It wasn't necessary to meet me at the airport yesterday.
[Use : needn't]
(a) It needn't to meet me at the airport yesterday.
(b) You needn't have met me at the airport yesterday.
(c) You needn't necessary to meet me at the airport yesterday.
(d) It needn't necessarily meet me at the airport yesterday.

(7) "Please teach me to cycle," she asked her brother.
[Rewrite in indirect form.........]
(a) She requested her brother to teach her to cycle.
(b) She made a request to her brother to teach her cycle.
(c) She requested her brother to please teach her to cycle.
(d) She made a request to her brother to please teach her cycle.

(8) The peasants regarded him as a thief and called him a villain.
[End : ....the peasants]
(a) He was regarded as a thief and called a villain by the peasants.
(b) He is regarded as a thief and called a villain by the peasants.
(c) He was being regarded as a thief and called a villain by the peasants.
(d) He was being regarded as a thief and was being called a villain by the peasants.

Answers *in Topper's Style*

1. (i) **The Lazy Donkey**

About a hundred years ago, there lived a kind and hardworking farmer. He had a special power by which he could understand the language of animals. One evening, he heard the donkey and the bull talking to each other. He hid behind a tree and listened. The bull was complaining to his friend, the donkey.

"I am very tired", he said, "I have worked so hard in the fields today."

"You don't need to work so much", replied the donkey. "Look at me - all I do the whole day is eat, sleep and enjoy myself!"

The bull thought that the donkey was very lucky. "What do I do to live like you?" he asked sadly.

"Well, I always pretend to be ill. Don't eat your food, moan and roll on the ground as if you are in pain. Then, the farmer won't take you to the fields", the donkey advised.

So, the next morning, the bull did exactly as the donkey had advised him. But, the farmer, who had heard everything, was determined to teach the lazy donkey a lesson. So, the farmer went to where the donkey was sitting and said aloud, "The bull is sick. It will cost a lot of money to buy its medicines and feed the donkey at the same time. This year, the crops weren't very good either. I'll keep the bull as he is a hardworking fellow but I will sell the donkey for some much needed cash."

As soon as the farmer went away, the donkey rushed to the bull and said, "Brother, I overheard the farmer say that he would give you antibiotics and no food which will make you all right."

"What are antibiotics?" asked the bull.

"Oh brother, it is the medicine which has a bitter taste. And what's more, you'll have no food at all", said the donkey. "If I were you, I would work hard instead of dying by drinking that medicine."

The bull agreed to work hard the next day because he was a simple minded animal. He thought, "Why die by drinking medicine with no food?"

The next day, both the donkey and the bull were looking fresh. The donkey had learned its lesson and the farmer made sure both had enough work from that day onwards.

(ii) **For the Motion**

According to a recent research in the UK, teenagers who spend more than 3 hours each day on social media sites are more than twice as likely to suffer poor mental health when compared to those who are not on social media. It seems that this may cause these children to delay their emotional and social development. According to the report, social media is potentially a source of social comparison, cyber bullying and isolation which could lead to mental health problems.

The results of a survey from a university in Scotland show that the use of social media particularly at night, with strong emotional involvement, leads to poorer sleep quality, lower self-esteem and higher levels of anxiety. This can be a problem as teenagers with low self-esteem tend to grow up as depressed adults. Besides these negative effects, we all know that social media is a distraction from their studies causing such teenagers to perform poorly in examinations. Also, it can become a serious addiction if they use social media too often. This can affect teenagers in a negative way by causing depression if they are not allowed to access social media for some length of time.

Teachers also observe that those teenagers who are members of social networks do not follow spelling and grammar rules in their school work as they have got used to using abbreviations commonly used on social media. Many children find it hard to differentiate between social networking communication and real world communication. In fact, many teachers are complaining that social networking communication with misspellings and lack of grammar are seeping through to student's school writings.

Another problem is that many social media sites such as Facebook, which give teenagers their own page having information only about them, make teenagers more self-centred. Such sites lead some vulnerable teenagers to think that everything revolves around them which further leads to emotional problems in their later life. This might also result in an inability to empathise with others.

Thus, it is clear that social networking has a bad effect on teenagers.

Against the Motion

Many parents think that teenagers can only misuse social networking sites. But, this is not true. Social networking sites are an easy way to communicate with other people. Only if we give too much exposure to these sites, will these sites become harmful.

It is very easy for parents to say that social networking causes problems with their teenagers. The nature of social networking is such that it has a positive effect on teenagers. When parents let it go out of control, it starts causing problems. So, parents should improve their method of parenting by giving more of their time and attention to their teenage children.

As they don't give enough time to their children, the teenagers resort to spending time on social networking. Spending time online is essential for young people to pick up the social and technical skills they need to be competent citizens in today's digital age. Teenagers must learn basic social and technical skills to fully participate in modern society. They learn to adapt to public socialising as well as managing an elaborate network of friends and acquaintances.

In addition, social networking brings teenagers more in touch with their peers. Young people are motivated to learn from their peers online. They interact and receive feedback from one another. They are motivated to learn more from each other than from adults. Teachers and adults are no longer the only sources of knowledge.

Another fact is that social networking is a must for teenagers as it is an important part of a teenager's life. It provides an avenue for them to express their feelings and interact with other teenagers. It also provides them with a source of information as to what other teenagers are going through and how to overcome difficulties in various fields. Not having access to social networking would isolate and limit their perspective on life.

There are many things in the world worse than social media that teenagers can get involved in. If social media is used correctly, it will definitely lead to better development of teenagers.

(iii) I remember the accident as if it happened yesterday. I was having a great time at a friend's birthday party. Soon, I had to leave because I had homework to do. My mother came to pick me up in the car. I sat in the back seat. I remember the weather that day: it was cold and rainy. I was looking out of the window the whole time while my mother drove. I went into a deep daydream thinking about my planned trip to the mall next day.

Suddenly, I felt an impact as if I had been hit very hard. My mother tried to stop our car as fast as she could but her foot slipped from the brake pedal and it was too late. The impact was so strong that it made me bang my head on the front seat. Suddenly, just as I thought it was all over, another vehicle came right behind us to hit us from the back. It was really painful. I lifted my head to look up and saw my mother; she was conscious but could not move.

Soon, I heard the siren from an approaching ambulance. They took my mother in the ambulance as it appeared that she had some major injury. Then, my uncle arrived to take me home. There was a lot of traffic on the road and the occupants of every car that passed by would stare at our damaged car as if the car was made of gold.

The next thing, I remember is that I woke up in my bed at home. The first thing on my mind was my mother. I rushed to her bedroom and found her sleeping in her bed. I was relieved and happy, my heart relaxed and I started breathing normally again. I went close to her and stared at her for a short amount of time examining her for injuries. There were only minor injuries. So, I got in her bed and went to sleep next to her.

(iv) I returned to my city after almost five years. A lot has changed in these years while I was completing my studies abroad. There have been several changes in Delhi's infrastructure including wider roads, fly overs and a wider network of Metro extending upto the NCR.

After coming out of the airport, I boarded a taxi which was very comfortable and fitted with AC and GPS. The taxi driver was speaking in English and then excused himself as he steered the vehicle to the side and answered his cell-phone. Delhi has changed considerably in the years. The most unexpected thing happened when the taxi driver asked me whether I would like to pay by cash or card. It was really good for me.

On my way, I noticed a network of wide-roads and fly overs. Moreover, broad green sign boards gave it an international standard and it really dazzled me.

What caught my attention was the tremendous progress made by the metro. More metro stations have come up and more metro lines have opened connecting far off destinations all over Delhi and NCR. I also noticed new sanitation facilities and public toilets constructed under Swach Bharat Abhiyan at different locations, and places have been kept clean and easily usable for all.

I also met some of my friends in the evening. They took me to the nearby mall.

As we passed through, I could see the market completely transformed, new modern hospitals have come up. Restaurants serving fast food and international cuisines with neon light and flashy sign boards covered the landscape. I treated my friends at a restaurant serving authentic Japanese cuisine. Everyone relished 'Sushi', the famous delicacy of Japan. I could observe that not only the attitude but people's taste has also changed. Five years ago, the only restaurant we used to go to was Pizza Hut or McDonald's. But now Swiggy, Ubereats and other food delivery apps have become common. Everything has changed except the pollution that envelops the city and the lack of woman safety which are two major areas where much improvement needs to be done.

(v) The word 'corruption' is not something we hear only in recent times. It has existed in our society since long. History reveals that it was present even in the Mauryan period. Great scholar Kautilya mentions the existence of forty types of corruption in his contemporary society. It was practised even in the Mughal and Sultanate period. When the East India Company took control of our country, corruption reached new heights.

Now-a-days, corruption in India has become so common that people are averse to thinking of public life without it. Corruption means illegal or dishonest behaviour, especially by people in positions of power.

In other words, undue favour for anyone for some monetary or other gains is corruption. Simultaneously, depriving the genuinely deserving of their right or privilege is also a corrupt practice. Giving up of one's duty is yet another form of corruption. Besides, thefts and misuse of public property constitute varieties of corruption.

Dishonesty, exploitation, malpractices, scams and scandals are various manifestations of corruption. It has spread its wings in every sphere of life namely business, administration, politics, officialdom and services. In fact, there is hardly any sector which can be called non-corrupt. Corruption is evidently present in every segment and every section of our society barring the social status attached to it.

To root out the evil of corruption from society, we need to make a comprehensive code of conduct for politicians and bureaucrats. Judiciary should be given more independence and initiatives on issues related to corruption.

Law and order machinery should be allowed to work without political interference. NGOs and media should come forward to create awareness against corruption in society and educate people on combatting this evil.

A non-corrupt society is a moral responsibility of every citizen, and we are morally bound to stand against corruption and fight against it and save our system from collapsing.

2. (i) ABC Public School,
Jayanagar,
Bengaluru 560070

23rd October, 20XX

The Secretary,
Ace Youth Hostel,
Mysuru 570001

Subject Request regarding accommodation for 2 days

Dear Sir,

This is to inform you that our school is sponsoring an overnight excursion of senior students to visit Mysuru and nearby areas on 10th and 11th November, 20XX. The group consists of 15 girls and 20 boys accompanied by two teachers. They will require overnight accommodation on the night of 10th November in Mysuru and will be reaching at 11 a.m. on the same day. They will stay for two days departing by 5 p.m. on the 11th November, 20XX. Two dormitories (bedroom) will be required for the students, one for girls and one for boys. The teachers will require separate single rooms. I wanted to enquire of your establishment can accomodate the group on these dates. If yes, I request you to send me your quotation of the costs for the same. If you require any further information, you may contact the undersigned on contact no. 97456XXXXX.

Thanking You,

Yours sincerely,
Sudhir
Head Boy

(ii)

B-147, Haripur Colony,
New Delhi 1100055

12th October, 20XX

My dear Shrawan,

I am grieved to hear from Ramesh about your dear mother's untimely demise; and, I can well imagine the great loss you have suffered. You have one consolation, however, that of having been the best son to her and of having given her the most devoted care during her long illness.

At a time like this, little can be said to comfort you and time alone will prepare you to deal with the loss. I feel that I have lost a great well wisher in her and indeed all who knew her cannot forget her as she was so kind, loving and caring.

Please accept my heartiest condolences on this tragic happening. I shall be meeting you very soon.

Your friend,
Kushal

3. (i) **CHRISTMAS MEET**

Activity Council Members Meeting

Date: Saturday, 4th July, 20XX

Time: 9 a.m. to 1 p.m.

Venue: Biology Lab, Room 35

The agenda of the meeting is :

- Discuss activities to be organised in the Christmas Fete
- Discuss cost and infrastructure required

Members are requested to come up with suggestions and ideas for the Fete.

(ii) **To** principal@stflorence.org

Subject Request to appoint judges for a talent search event.

Dear Sir/Ma'am,

I am Avantika, the Activity Coordinator of the Student Council, St. Agnes' School. We are conducting a talent search contest for the students of Classes VIII, IX and X. This is to be held on the 25 December, 20XX from 9 a.m. to 4 p.m. in Music, Art, Dance, Magic, Acrobatics and Stand-up Comedy.

We request you to send a team of three teachers from your school to judge the talent search, Everybody's Got Talent.

Anticipating a positive response,

Yours faithfully,
Avantika
Activity Coordinator

4. (i) (1) (a) grant to support a student's education
(2) (d) displeased as her hopes have not been fulfilled

(ii) (b) destination

(iii) (a) Lucie took admission to the University of Versailles for the following reasons :
1. The University offered her a scholarship to study Computer Science and get a degree.
2. Her friend Josephine studies there and Lucie can share the apartment where she stays.

(b) Lucie consoles herself by saying that Versailles has several attractions, besides being only a few minutes away by train from Paris.
Her sorrow is that she has to live in Versailles instead of Paris where she would have liked to stay.

(c) Lucie says these words to herself because she is much relieved to have finally reached where she is going to live for the next one year. It was her dream to live in Paris which has been fulfilled now.

(d) Girls say 'hello' in France by giving each other two kisses, guys by giving girls two kisses and guys by shaking each other's hands.

(e) Lucie is ready for the future, all alone in a new country.

(iv) On entering, the hallway was painted red on the walls and black on the roof. The floor was wooden. On the left was the telephone on a table and, further on, a bathroom. On the right are two rooms with Josephine's room being the first and Lucie's room the second one.

5. (i) (1) made (2) picked
(3) are grown (4) bear
(5) have been gathered (6) roasted
(7) gives (8) grounded

(ii) (a) till/until/at (b) from (c) to/till (d) since
(e) in (f) at (g) with (h) between

(iii) (1) (c) Alice seems quite intelligent; nonetheless, she often gets poor grades. (Nonetheless is used to connect two contrasting ideas.)
(2) (a) This restaurant has some of the best chefs in the town; moreover, their service is excellent.
(3) (c) I've never been to the US in spite of having friends and relatives there.
(4) (b) Though he is a reckless driver, he hasn't had any accidents.

(iv) (1) (b) Your horse is not as well trained as this.
(2) (c) The children won't sit out in the garden if the weather is hot.
(3) (c) The thief ran too fast to be caught by the police.
(4) (d) Her attitude is often the cause of my annoyance.
(5) (c) You should not have talked to her like that.
(6) (b) You needn't have met me at the airport yesterday.
(7) (a) She requested her brother to teach her to cycle.
(8) (a) He was regarded as a thief and called a villain by the peasants.

SQP Code : **PB-6/10** Series ***i*-Succeed 6-25/10** Roll No.

Sample Question Paper 06

English Language 10th (Code 01)

General Instructions

1. You will not be allowed to write during the first 15 minutes. This time is to be spent in reading the question paper.
2. The time given at the head of this paper is the time allowed for writing the answers.
3. Attempt all five questions.
4. The intended marks for questions or parts of questions are given in brackets [].
5. You are advised to spend not more than 30 minutes in answering Question 1 and 20 minutes in answering Question 2.

Time : 2 Hrs.

Max. Marks : 80

Question 1.

(Do not spend more than 30 minutes on this question.)

Write a composition (300-350 words) on **any one** of the following. [20]

(i) Write an original story starting with the words 'It was a dark windy night….'

(ii) 'Academic excellence is the only requirement for a successful career.'
Express your views for or against this statement.

(iii) You have to go to your home town due to demise of your grandfather. Write an account of your experience of travelling over a long distance (overnight) in an unreserved second class compartment.

(iv) You recently read a novel which was quite engrossing due to different characters. Describe your favourite character and give reason why you like this character.

(v) Study the picture given below. Write a story or a description or an account of what it suggests to you. Your composition may be about the subject of the picture or you may take suggestions from it; however, there must be a clear connection between the picture and your composition.

Question 2.

(Do not spend more than 20 minutes on this question.)

Select **any one** of the following. [10]

(i) You had taken an Annual Maintenance Contract from M/s Cool Service Agency, Panchkula for maintenance of the 16 Samsung air conditioners installed in your office in Sector 7, Chandigarh. However, the service is irregular and unsatisfactory. Write a complaint letter to the proprietor of the agency. Invent the necessary details. You are Dev Arora, Punjab Coaching Institute, Sector 7, Chandigarh.

(ii) Write a letter to your neighbour, Ms Hooda, apologising to her on breaking of her window glass by your son. You are BS Chaudhary.

Question 3.

(i) Your school is arranging an Inter-School Singing Competition for patriotic songs to be sung by groups of students on the occasion of Independence Day. Write a notice for your school notice board inviting names of all the interested student groups so that the team to represent the school may be finalised. [5]

(ii) Write an e-mail to the Principal of one of the schools to request him/her to send a team for participation in the Inter-School Singing Competition. [5]

Question 4.

Read the following passage carefully and answer the questions that follow.

I rested for a moment at the door of Anand Bhavan, on Market Road, where coffee drinkers and tiffin eaters at their tables sat **transfixed**, uttering low moans on seeing me. I wanted to assure them, 'Don't fear, I am not out to trouble you. Eat your tiffin in peace, don't mind me. You, nearest to me, hugging the cash box, you are craven with fear, afraid even to breathe. Go on, count the cash, if that's your pleasure. I just want to watch that's all. If my

tail trails down to the street, if I am blocking your threshold, it is because, I'm told, I'm eleven feet tip to tail. I can't help it. I'm not out to kill. I'm too full. I found a green pasture teeming with food on the way. I won't need any for several days to come, won't stir, not until I feel hungry again. Tigers attack only when they feel hungry, unlike human beings who slaughter one another without purpose or hunger.

SP-06

To the great delight of children, schools were being hurriedly closed. Children of all ages and sizes were running **helter–skelter** screaming joyously, "No school, no school. Tiger, tiger!" They were shouting and laughing and even enjoying being scared. They seemed to welcome me.

I felt like joining them. So, I bounded away from the restaurant door and trotted along

with them, at which they cried, "The tiger is coming to eat us; let us get back to the school!" I followed them through their school gate while they ran up and shut themselves in the school hall securely. I ascended the steps of the school, saw an open door at the far end of a veranda, and walked in. It happened to be the headmaster's room, I believe, as I noticed a very dignified man jumping on his table and heaving himself up into an attic. I walked in and flung

myself on the cool floor, having a partiality for cool stone floors, with

my head under the large desk– which gave me the feeling of being back in the Mempi cave. As I dozed, I was aware of cautious steps and hushed voices all around. I was in no mood to be bothered about anything. All I wanted was a little moment of sleep; the daylight was dazzling. In a half sleep, I heard the doors of the room being shut, bolted and locked.

I didn't care. I slept.

While I slept a great deal of consultation was going on. I learnt about it later through my master, who was in the crowd which had gathered after making sure that I had been properly locked up–and was watching. The headmaster seems to have remarked some days later "Never dreamt in my wildest mood that I'd have to yield my place to a tiger…"A wag had retorted, "Might be one way of maintaining better discipline among the boys."

'Now that this brute is safely locked up, we must decide', began a teacher. At this moment, my master pushed his way through the crowds and admonished them. "Never use the words 'beast' or 'brute'. They're ugly words coined by humans in their arrogance. Human beings think all other creatures are 'beasts'. Awful word!"

(i) For each word given below, choose the correct meaning (as used in the passage) from the options provided. [2]

(1) *transfixed* (line 2)

(a) mesmerised
(b) to be enchanted
(c) conflicted or confused
(d) pierced into something

(2) *helter-skelter* (line 12)

(a) slowly
(b) running
(c) quickly in disorderly fashion
(d) strolling

(ii) Which word in the passage means the opposite of the word 'praised'? [1]

(a) cautioned (b) admonished (c) arrogance (d) coinedt

(iii) Answer the following questions briefly in your own words.

(a) What reassurance did the tiger give the coffee drinkers? [2]

(b) In what way are tigers different from human beings? [2]

(c) Which sentences tell us that the tiger's owner had great respect for the tiger? [2]

(d) What did the headmaster say some days later? [2]

(e) Why were the children delighted? [1]

(iv) In not more than 50 words, describe the tiger's activities from the time it followed the school children till it slept. [8]

Question 5.

(i) Fill in each of the numbered blanks with correct form of the words given in brackets. Do not copy the passage but write in correct serial order the word or phrase appropriate to the blank space. [4]

Example I ……(0)…… (met) him in the mall the day before yesterday.

Answer (0) had met

Sago pudding is a popular Chinese dessert often served in many Chinese restaurants. The dessert is made of pearl sago which is almost transparent and it ......**(1)**...... (swell) during cooking.

Sago can ......**(2)**...... (obtain) from the trunks of the sago palm which are found in swamps. The palm reaches a height of about ninety metres when fully ......**(3)**...... (grow). The palms ......**(4)**......(cut down) just before they flower. Part of the trunk ......**(5)**...... (pound) into pulp before it ......**(6)**...... (turn) into powder by a machine.

The powder is later washed and ......**(7)**...... (dry). It is now called sago flour. This flour is then kneaded into dough and ......**(8)**...... (pass) through another machine to form the pearl-like grains which we see in sago pudding.

(ii) Fill in each blank with appropriate word. [4]

(a) Most people left the party .... 2 AM.

(b) The party went on .... 4 AM.

(c) I've taken a resolution not to drink .... the end of year.

(d) I'll return your money .... the end of the year.

(e) Because I had to reach home before dinner, I could stay with my friends .... just two hours.
(f) I liked the book so much that I finished it .... a day.
(g) There was a security alert .... the airport.
(h) .... a pause in the conversation, I excused myself and left for home.

(iii) Join the following sentences to make one complete sentence **without using and, but** or **so**. Choose the correct option. [4]

(1) The lawyer defended his client very well. He lost the case.
(a) Though the lawyer defended his client very well, yet he lost the case.
(b) Although the lawyer defended his client very well but he lost the case.
(c) Though the lawyer defended his client very well, he lost the case.
(d) None of the above

(2) The bus left at six o' clock. We arrived at the bus stop at five past six.
(a) The bus had left after we arrived at the bus stop.
(b) The bus had came after we arrived at the bus stop.
(c) The bus had left before we arrived at the bus stop.
(d) The bus had come before we arrived at the bus stop.

(3) The beggar was crossing the road. The accident took place then.
(a) The accident took place and the beggar was crossing the road.
(b) The beggar was crossing the road yet the accident took place.
(c) Although the accident took place, the beggar was crossing the road.
(d) The accident took place while the beggar was crossing the road.

(4) She studied German for three years. Then, she moved to Berlin.
(a) After she had studied German for three years, she moved to Berlin.
(b) After she moved to Berlin, she studied German for three years.
(c) After having studied German for three years, she moved to Berlin.
(d) Both (a) and (c)

(iv) Choose the correct option to rewrite the following according to instructions given after each sentence. [8]

(1) The only person I didn't see was Geeta.
[Use : except]
(a) I saw no one except Geeta.
(b) I saw everyone except Geeta.
(c) Except Geeta, I saw nothing.
(d) Except Geeta, I saw something.

SP-06

(2) Manisha decided to visit her friend and tell her the sad news.
[Use : drop]
(a) Manisha decided to drop at on her friend and tell her the sad news.
(b) Manisha decided to drop on her friend and tell her the sad news.
(c) Manisha decided to drop in on her friend and tell her the sad news.
(d) Manisha decided for dropping at on her friend and tell her the sad news.

(3) In spite of bad weather, a huge crowd came to see the match.
[Begin with : The bad weather]
(a) The bad weather deterred the huge crowd from coming to see the match.
(b) The bad weather didn't deter the huge crowd from coming to see the match.
(c) The bad weather hadn't deter the huge crowd from coming to see the match.
(d) The bad weather did deter the huge crowd from coming to see the match.

(4) He decided to walk instead of taking a taxi.
[Begin with : Rather than]
(a) Rather than not taking a taxi, he decided to walk.
(b) Rather than not taking a taxi, he decided not to walk.
(c) Rather than taking a taxi, he decided to walk.
(d) Rather than taking a taxi, he decided not to walk.

(5) As soon as the bus arrived, all rushed to their seats.
[Rewrite using : hardly]
(a) Hardly the bus arrived, when all rushed to their seats.
(b) Hardly had the bus arrived, when all rushed to their seats.
(c) Hardly had the bus arrived, than all rushed to their seats.
(d) Hardly did the bus arrived, than all rushed to their seats.

(6) To the best of my knowledge, he is a vegetarian.
[Begin with : As far...]
(a) As far my knowledge, he is a vegetarian. (b) As far my knowledge, he is not a vegetarian.
(c) As far as I know, he is not a vegetarian. (d) As far as I know, he is a vegetarian.

(7) He must fill in the form.
[Begin with : The form...]
(a) The form should be filled by him. (b) The form could be filled in by him.
(c) The form will be filled by him. (d) The form must be filled in by him.

(8) The doctor said to the patient, 'Quit Smoking.'
[Report the given sentence]
(a) The doctor told the patient to quit smoking.
(b) The doctor requested the patient to quit smoking.
(c) The doctor advised the patient to quit smoking.
(d) The doctor said to the patient to quit smoking.

Answers *in Topper's Style*

1. (i) It was a dark windy night. I was on my way from the bus station to the main city square where I lived with one more associate. The cold air was biting and sharp, and I pulled up my scarf further up to the chin covering myself with my overcoat. I quickened my steps towards the area which was better lit and crowded. Unfortunately, no one was on the road and, on one corner of the square, a suspicious type of man was standing staring at me. My heartbeat increased and my steps quickened as I could get no vehicle/taxi to reach my house. I wanted to go home and into my warm bed as quickly as possible.

After the first few steps, I realised I was being followed. An obscure looking man, covered in an overcoat, his shining hair reminding me that he was not close to being a gentle man, filled me with scary thoughts.
I started walking very quickly realising that I was in danger, looking here and there for any sign of human being in that lonely windy right. I was alone, I shivered trying to hide myself behind my scarf and coat as I kept going feeling the reassuring grip around my cell inside my right pocket and purse on the left side inside my coat.

Then, he called me to stop. I just could not breathe but he called after me, 'Madam, please stop!'
He started by saying that there was no reason to feel scared or shiver out of fright as he was not a murderer or 'goon'. Two days ago, his wife had died. She resembled so much to me so he was staring at me and trying to reason out if his dead wife could come back to life. I didn't know how to react after listening to his words but I picked up courage and replied, "I am Rosa Lyndon and I work for Siemens Private Ltd." I told him to go home and live with the good memories of his dead wife instead of following and staring at someone. He turned and started going in another direction and I thanked God that I was safe and alive.

(ii) **For the Motion**

I will start with a quote, "The beautiful thing about learning is that no one can take it from you." Right to Education is a Fundamental Right of every child in the age group of six to fourteen years. The education system in the primary years is designed so as to provide basic knowledge on each subject and help the youth of today in choosing their subject of interest for its deeper study in higher classes.

This part of education can only be provided effectively through universities. It plays a key role in the development of society and the nation. In fact, information cannot be converted into knowledge without education.

Education makes us capable of interpreting things. It helps in raising future leaders by providing them clear understanding and developing their decision-making abilities. It makes them resourceful and competent. Excellence in academics prepares students for the competition ahead and teaches them to work hard as well.

Academic qualifications may not be enough on their own to ensure success but they indicate that the person who possesses them has got the necessary knowledge required. Conversely, imagine a new world order in education, where people don't study beyond school, but join their business or look for jobs straight after school, with no higher qualifications which certify their worth. Then, how would employers choose between them?

Thus, higher academic achievement is important because, in order to do well in academics for obtaining a degree or other qualification, students have to work hard, master new skills and learn a great deal of specialised knowledge. These are all valuable attributes for success in any field which is why employers value academic qualifications. Getting admission in a good college indicates to a future employer that the student is better than many others. Further, academic excellence will ensure admission to the best universities for higher education which provide exposure to a variety of knowledge; thus, giving an excellent start to the student's career.

Therefore, all these arguments prove that academic excellence is the only requirement for a successful career.

Against the Motion

A well-known saying tells us, "The goal of education is to raise the leaders of tomorrow." But, then how is it that most of the leaders and successful persons today happen to be college dropouts? Both Steve Jobs, founder of Apple, and Bill Gates, founder of Microsoft, are in this category. This is because having degrees cannot ensure success. Education today fails to impart necessary life skills and polish the personality of an individual. For these, students have to attend specialised workshops or training sessions.

Education will surely give you an overview of a subject but it fails to provide an overview of how the world works. It does not ensure mastery of skills and competencies. It tells people what to think instead of how to think. The end result is that society now has just robots who have switched their minds off only to believe what is being taught. One's attitude towards life is what brings success in a career. Undoubtedly, academic excellence can provide you degrees or may even land you a job but your success depends upon how you think, behave, walk, talk and present yourself.

Many successful college dropouts have proved that prosperity does not depend upon academic qualifications but upon opportunities provided by entrepreneurs who may not necessarily be highly educated. Successful entrepreneurs even benefit from not having academic qualifications because going to college and taking examinations forces people to learn and think like millions of other graduates. This actually makes it less likely that they will come up with the truly mould-breaking insights and 'disruptive' ideas on which successful innovations and new business models are built.

Unfortunately, the materialistic world has changed the concept of success.

It has become a rat-race where every student chases grades and therefore the entire perception of success and prosperity has changed. Rather than studying to reach our full potential, we do it because we think it is necessary for a successful career. Even after that, we may find ourselves in the wrong profession and lacking job satisfaction.

Thus, academic excellence is in no way the only requirement for a successful career.

(iii) I once had the misfortune to travel over a long distance, about 2000 km, in an unreserved second class train compartment. It was truly a misfortune as I was sitting cramped in one seat for about 41 hours at a stretch in a crowded coach while travelling from Guwahati to Delhi.

As my journey was planned at short notice due to sudden demise of my grandfather, I had failed to get a confirmed reservation. The only way I could travel in the train in an unreserved compartment was to bribe a licensed porter on the platform to find a seat for me. Thus, for ₹ 100 extra, I was able to get a seat although it was in the middle of a long seat with two persons sitting on either side of me. Sometime after the train left Guwahati, I dozed off as I had not slept properly the previous night. When I woke up, it was the next morning and we were approaching Katihar. I suddenly realised that I should check whether my suitcase was still where I had kept it.

I was relieved to see that it was still under the seat. Some of the passengers were different as the train had stopped at 6 or 7 stations so far. I used the toilet and returned to my seat.

However, one sight in our compartment disturbed me a lot. A lady passenger with an infant was sitting in on one of the seats opposite mine. The infant had dirtied the compartment but the lady did not bother to clean up the mess. However, she had cleaned and washed the infant in the toilet and put new clothes on it so that it was fast asleep. When I suggested to the lady that a nasty smell had permeated the compartment and she should clean up the mess created by her baby, she retorted that the sweeper at the next station would do so. I had no alternative but to keep my nose closed for as long as I could!

The rest of the journey passed uneventfully and I reached Delhi the next morning. What a terribly tiring journey it was!

(iv) **My Favourite Character in a Novel**

My favourite character is the tomboy, nicknamed 'Scout', in the novel 'To Kill a Mockingbird' by Harper Lee. She is an important character in the novel as she helps narrate the story. She is only nine years old when the novel starts. I like her because she describes her thoughts and feelings about the events that happen. She develops the plot and theme very graphically so that the reader can almost picture every scene. She is a daughter to a single father, a sister to her elder brother and a friend to her cousin, Dill.

Her real name is Jean-Louis but, since she is a tomboy, she prefers the friendship with boys instead of girls. She likes to prove that she can be as good as a boy with her actions. During the course of the novel she matures just like her brother Jem, who is now going through the difficult age of adolescence.

The story revolves around the trial of an African-American who is accused of raping a Caucasian woman. Scout's father is the defendant's lawyer and proves to the jury that the defendant did not rape the victim. In fact, the victim also admits that he did not do so. However, the jury is so much biased against African-Americans that they still declare the defendant guilty of the crime. Ultimately, the defendant is shot by the prison guards when he was trying to escape.

All these events have a long-lasting effect on Scout who realises the depth of bias against African-Americans. She also realises the good qualities her father possesses as he is neither biased against African-Americans nor afraid of anybody. He agreed to defend an African-American against the system of justice biased against them.

Scout faces so many issues in the duration of the novel but one of the most lingering issues for her is the question of what it means 'to be a lady.' Oddly enough, the women in her life impose more rigid requirements on her than men do. Scout's tomboyishness drives Aunt Alexandria to distraction; Miss Caroleno sees Scout's outspokenness and honesty as impertinence. But in the end, when she explains why the Sheriff can't charge Boo with Bob Ewell's murder, she has become the kind of person who makes her father very-very proud. She is truly an admirable character and is thus my favourite.

(v) **Floods in our Village**

I live in a small village on the left bank of the Ghaghra River in Bahraich district. Every year, during the rainy season, our village is surrounded by the river water. So, we have built our houses on rocky ground much above the level of the surrounding areas. Last year, due to heavy rains, we were forced to evacuate our village by using boats as there were big sheets of water all around. It was a horrible sight.

We went to our relatives' farm in the interior about 10 km away where we were safe. On the way, we saw other villages submerged in water with people sitting on their rooftops waiting to be rescued. Some people were carrying their luggage in the boats sent by the government for moving the residents to safer places. The Indian Army had been called out to help in the movement of people. The soldiers helped the elderly, the infirm and children to get into the boats safely.

The government officers had made an arrangement for a big relief camp on high ground. Most of the residents had been temporarily shifted there. A community kitchen was being run for the camp residents. Further, clean drinking water was available to save the camp residents from the possible attack of water-borne diseases. They were also given medical aid if required.

The floods caused great loss to the people in the affected areas. The standing crops were completely washed away. In our village, nearly all the mud houses were washed away by the swift current of water. Hundreds of cattle were drowned.

When the water receded after about ten days, we returned to our village to find that some walls of our home were damaged by the swirling water. These walls required extensive repair. We applied for and received some funds from the government for repairing the walls which was a great relief.

We were also able to get a loan from the government for buying seeds and chemical fertilisers for the next crop. The government has promised us that, this year, an embankment will be constructed along the river banks near our village to prevent floods in the future.

2. Punjab Coaching Institute,
Madhya Marg, Sector 7,
Chandigarh - 160007

7th May, 20XX

The Proprietor,
M/s Cool Service Agency,
Sector 4,
Panchkula - 134112

Subject Complaint regarding irregular service

Dear Sir,

This is to inform you that we had taken an AMC (Annual Maintenance Contract) for our 16 Samsung air conditioners with your agency under contract no. AMC 23/17 on 15th March, 20XX. At the time, we were assured by your Marketing Executive that your service engineer would carry out a monthly preventive maintenance visit in the first week of every month and any other complaints registered by us will be promptly attended to within one day.

Unfortunately, the preventive maintenance monthly visit for May has not been held so far. Last month, two of our complaints got unsatisfactory response from your side as they were attended after 4-5 days. This is causing great inconvenience to us. Our students have started complaining and threatening to boycott classes due to the discomfort during summer.

You are requested to take action at the earliest so as to honour the terms of the AMC; otherwise, we will be compelled to go to the consumer forum for redressal.

Yours faithfully,
Dev Arora
Manager

2. (ii) K-8, Raja Surajmal Vihar,
Bhiwani, Haryana

20th February, 20XX

Dear Ms Hooda,

I came to know that my younger son has broken a window in your house while playing in the street. I hope no one was hurt due to the crash. I am extremely sorry for my son's carelessness. I apologise for the damage caused by him. I request you to please send me the bill for the repairs.

I assure you that such incidence will not take place again as I have taken my son to task and scolded him to be very careful in the future. If there is anything else I can do for you, please let me know. Once again, apologies for the damage and my son's carelessness.

Yours sincerely,
BS Chaudhary

3. (i)

Singing Stars – Swatantrata Special

Inter-School Singing Competition – Auditions
on 10th August, 20XX
from 11:00 a.m. onwards
in the Auditorium, St. Xavier High School

All the student groups who wish to participate should submit their names to the Head Boy latest by 6th August, 20XX.

(ii) **To** principal@stjosephschool.org

Subject Invitation for Participation in the Inter-School Singing Competition

Respected Sir/Ma'am,

This is to inform you that our school is arranging an Inter-School Singing Competition for patriotic songs to be sung by a group of students on the occasion of Independence Day. Suitable prizes will be awarded to the three best student groups.

The actual competition will be held on Saturday 13th August, 20XX, from 10 : 00 AM onwards in our school auditorium. Participation by students of your school will make a huge impact on the student community as a whole. So, you are requested to send a group of students to participate in the competition.

We anticipate a positive response from you to make this function a success. You are welcome to contact me for any clarification.

Thanking you,

Yours faithfully,
Ajit Arora
Head Boy
St. Xavier High School
Mobile No. 98876XXXXX

4. (i) (1) (a) mesmerised
(2) (c) quickly in disorderly fashion

(ii) (b) admonished

(iii) (a) The tiger reassured the coffee drinkers that he did not want to trouble them. They could eat their tiffin in peace and should not be afraid of him.
(b) Tigers attack only when they feel hungry, unlike human beings,who slaughter one another without purpose or hunger. In this way, tigers are different from human beings.
(c) The last four sentences of the passage, in which the tiger's owner said that we should never use words such as 'beast' or 'brute' for the tiger, tell us that he had great respect for the tiger and the wildlife. He said that such words showed human's arrogance.
(d) Some days later, the headmaster said that he was shocked and scared to see a tiger in his office.
He also said that he had never dreamt in his wildest mood that he would have to give his place to a tiger.
(e) The children were delighted because school was closed due to the presence of the tiger there. Thus, they had a holiday.

(iv) Following the children, the tiger stepped inside the school gate, saw an open door and entered it.
On seeing the tiger, the headmaster jumped up into the attic above. The tiger flung himself on to the cool stone floor with his head under the headmaster's desk and slept as the daylight was dazzling him and he wanted to relax for sometime.

5. (i) (1) swells (2) be obtained (3) grown (4) are cut down
(5) is pounded (6) is turned (7) dried (8) passed

(ii) (a) by (b) until (c) until/till (d) by
(e) for (f) in (g) at (h) During

(iii) (1) (c) Though the lawyer defended his client very well, he lost the case.
(2) (c) The bus had left before we arrived at the bus stop.
(3) (d) The accident took place while the beggar was crossing the road.
(4) (d) Both (a) and (c)

(iv) (1) (b) I saw everyone except Geeta.
(2) (c) Manisha decided to drop in on her friend and tell her the sad news.
(3) (b) The bad weather didn't deter the huge crowd from coming to see the match.
(4) (c) Rather than taking a taxi, he decided to walk.
(5) (b) Hardly had the bus arrived, when all rushed to their seats.
(6) (d) As far as I know, he is a vegetarian.
(7) (d) The form must be filled in by him.
(8) (c) The doctor advised the patient to quit smoking.

SQP Code : **PB-7/10** Series ***i*-Succeed 7-25/10** Roll No. [ ]

Sample Question Paper 07

English Language 10th (Code 01)

General Instructions

1. You will not be allowed to write during the first 15 minutes. This time is to be spent in reading the question paper.
2. The time given at the head of this paper is the time allowed for writing the answers.
3. Attempt all five questions.
4. The intended marks for questions or parts of questions are given in brackets [].
5. You are advised to spend not more than 30 minutes in answering Question 1 and 20 minutes in answering Question 2.

Time : 2 Hrs.

Max. Marks : 80

Question 1.

(Do not spend more than 30 minutes on this question.)

Write a composition (300-350 words) on **any one** of the following. [20]

(i) Write an original story entitled 'Lost and Found'.

(ii) "Old age homes are not necessary."
Express your views for or against this statement.

(iii) Think of a time when you found yourself in an embarrassing, situation. Narrate how you got into that situation, how you dealt with it and the lesson you learnt from it.

(iv) You have gone to a foreign country for your higher studies after graduation. You find that the city you live in is totally different from the Metro city you were living in back home. Describe your personal views about the differences.

(v) Study the picture given below. Write a story or description or an account of what it suggests to you. Your composition may be about the subject of the picture or you may take suggestion from it; however, there must be a clear connection between the picture and your composition.

Question 2.

(Do not spend more than 20 minutes on it.)

Select **any one** of the following. [10]

(i) You are Rajat Kumar, a resident of 79, Sector 4, Sector RK Puram, New Delhi. You are interested in joining the course in Communication Skills advertised by the Elite School of Language, South Extension–II. Write a letter of enquiry for the same.

(ii) Write a letter to your friend, Suresh, who has recently lost his job sympathising with him and encouraging to have better times in future. You are Aditya.

Question 3.

(i) You are the Cultural Secretary of your school. You have been asked to inform students about an Inter-House Dramatics Competition. Draft a notice in not more than 50 words with necessary details. [5]

(ii) Write an email to the Principal requesting him to make a decision regarding the prize to be awarded to the participants in the Inter-House Dramatics Competition. [5]

Question 4.

Read the following passage carefully and answer the questions that follows.

Curious as it may sound, I have always felt I am an Indian by accident. Let me explain why I say this. I was born in Bhagalpur. This ought to make me a Bihari. But I am not one because my mother was a Bengali whose family had settled in Bihar. Within weeks of being born I came to Calcutta, where I spent all my growing up years. My school was founded by a Frenchman, a soldier of fortune. And though I scored far better marks in Bengali and Hindi there, the only language I learnt was English.

How and why I have no clue, since we all spoke Bengali at home. My first English article appeared in the Statesman when I was 13. Soon, I published my first book of poems, again in English. I dropped out of college.

I wrote more books till the desire to change the world (yes, in those days we actually thought we could) brought me to what was then Bombay, to be a journalist.

Mumbai is where I have lived for most of my life. In between, for what seemed like six long years, I also lived in Lutyens' Delhi. In a charming bungalow just opposite the BJP office on Ashoka Road, eating subsidised meals in Parliament and representing Maharashtra's interests on a Shiv Sena ticket. So, am I a Mumbaikar? Or a Bengali from Calcutta? A Bihari? Or a born again Anglophile like Nirad C Chaudhari? I have no clue. Most Indians are like me, put together by accident. That's the magic of being a migrant in your own land, trying to discover your many identities.

My mother's maiden name seemed to suggest that someone in her family in the past had Muslim connection though her first name was Hindu (or Bengali, depending on how you see it). The only place of worship I ever saw her visit was the St Paul's cathedral on New Year's eve more out of convention than faith. My father was born a Hindu and his family home was in Kalighat. His father remarried and **chucked** them out. My father, his mother and two sisters found themselves on the street trying to fend for themselves, when a passing Jesuit took pity on them. He gave them shelter in Bishnupur where he ran a school. The freedom struggle brought my parents together. They married and we three brothers were born.

Never did it once strike me what my religion was, which state I belonged to, what my language ought to be, which culture I should fight for.

My adolescent years were spent in protesting against the Russians **invading** Czechoslovakia and the Americans in Vietnam. My Bengali DNA I guess, if you look around you, you will find many people like me who, in the midst of their many identities, accidentally chanced upon their Indianness. Each of them will swear by their regional culture, the language they speak, the faith they follow or (like me) do not. And, as they wander through all these, and discover themselves, they also discover the magic of being Indian.

(i) For each word given below, choose the correct meaning (as used in the passage) from the options provided. [2]

(1) *chucked* (line 23)
(a) kept aside
(b) threw
(c) retained in the same way
(d) throw up

(2) *invading* (line 30)
(a) conquering
(b) taking
(c) occupying
(b) Both (a) and (c)

(ii) Which word in the passage means the opposite of the word 'deliberately'? [1]
(a) curious
(b) accidentally
(c) together
(d) All of these

(iii) Answer the following questions briefly using your own words.

(a) Why does the author say that he is an Indian by accident? [2]

(b) What brought the author to Bombay? [2]

(c) Which quality in himself does the author attribute to his Bengali DNA? [2]

(d) What similarity does the author seem to have with Nirad C Chaudhuri as mentioned in the passage? [2]

(e) What did the passing Jesuit on road do to the author's family? [1]

(iv) Write, in your own words not exceeding 50, how the author discovers the magic of being Indian. [8]

Question 5.

(i) Fill in each of the numbered blanks with correct form of the words given in brackets. Do not copy the passage, but write in correct serial order the word or phrase appropriate to the blank space. [4]

Example She ......**(0)**...... (scream) at me for taking her book.

Answer (0) screamed

Peter was driving towards Punggol Point when he ...**(1)**... (lose) control of his vehicle. He was ...**(2)**... (meet) a friend to go water skiing. However, he ...**(3)**... (not have) a good time that day.

At track 13, a car ...**(4)**... (shoot) into his lane. In order to ...**(5)**... (avoid) the car, Peter ...**(6)**... (slam) the brakes. He ...**(7)**... (destine) not to escape unhurt. His car ...**(8)**... (spin), hit the kerb and then overturned. Peter hit his head against the steering wheel and blacked out.

(ii) Fill in each blank with appropriate words. [4]

(a) The phone bill has to be paid ...... Friday.
(b) Don't pay the bill today. Wait ...... tomorrow.
(c) What time do you usually arrive ...... work?
(d) He wiped his face ...... a tissue.
(e) Show me what's there ...... your bag.
(f) You can return my car ...... the end of the month.
(g) There were many interruptions ...... the chief guest's speech.
(h) I've to leave for office ...... 8:30 a.m.

(iii) Join the following sentences to make one complete sentence **without using and, but** or **so.** Choose the correct option. [4]

(1) The minister was wise. The king did not trust him.
(a) Though the minister was wise but the king did not trust him
(b) Though the minister was wise yet the king did not trust him.

(c) Though the minister was wise, the king did not trust him.
(d) None of the above

(2) We reached the port. The storm came on.
(a) Since we reached the port, the storm came on.
(b) When we reached the port, the storm came on.
(c) Unless we reached the port, the storm came on.
(d) All of the above

(3) One should not borrow money. One should not lend money.
(a) One should either borrow or land money.
(b) One should neither borrow nor lend money.
(c) One should borrow or lend money.
(d) Don't borrow or lend money.

(4) She will win the prize. She deserves it.
(a) She deserves it as she will win the prize.
(b) She deserves if since she will win the prize.
(c) She will win the prize when she deserves it.
(d) She will win the prize as she deserves it.

(iv) Choose the correct option to rewrite the following according to the instructions given after each sentence. [8]

(1) I don't listen to rap music at all. [Rewrite using : never]
(a) I don't never listen to rap music.
(b) I never not listen to rap mucis.
(c) I never listen to rap music.
(d) I never ever listen to rap music.

(2) This isn't my book. [Rewrite using : belong]
(a) The book doesn't belong to me.
(b) The book belongs to me.
(c) The book does belong to me.
(d) None of these

(3) The baby is awake at the moment. [Rewrite using : sleep]
(a) The baby is not sleeping at the moment.
(b) The baby is sleeping at the moment.
(c) The baby sleeps at the moment.
(d) The baby sleep at the moment.

(4) What is your opinion about this school? [Rewrite using : think]
(a) What did you think of this school?
(b) What you thought of this school?
(c) What do you think of this school?
(d) What you think of this school?

(5) I left and then they arrived. [Rewrite using : by the time]
(a) I left by the time they arrived.
(b) They arrived by the time I left.
(c) I had left by the time they arrived.
(d) They arrived by the time I had left.

(6) Sam fell during the football game. [Rewrite using : while]
(a) While Sam fell during the football game.
(b) Sam fell while playing football.
(c) Sam fell during the football game while.
(d) Both (b) and (c)

(7) They will not ask him. [Begin with : He...]
(a) He will be asked by them.
(b) He will not be asked by them.
(c) He will be by them asked.
(d) All of these

(8) He said, 'They will be arriving here by the next train.' [Begin with : He said that…]
(a) He said that they would be arriving there by the next train.
(b) He said that they would be arriving here by the next train.
(c) He said that they will be arriving here by the next train.
(d) He said that they will be arriving there by the next train.

Answers in Topper's Style

1. (i)

Lost and Found

The graveyard was cold, dark and dreary. One weary old oak tree leaned over the entrance gate and broken, battered headstones were scattered all around. I could hear the sound of the howling wind, and the creak and groan of branches as they swayed in the storm. The smell of fear and rotting leaves filled my nostrils. I breathed deeply afraid that I would get sick. As I walked towards my brother's grave, I heard another noise. It was of slow heavy footsteps. When I turned back, a tall muscular man was walking towards me. "I don't think this is a good idea", I shouted. "It's too late to change your mind", the man replied in a low threatening voice. "Either we dig him up now or you spend the rest of your life wondering how he died." "Ok, Ok", I mumbled.

I could still remember the day those two army officers arrived at my house to tell me that my brother was dead. I lost my brother. Their cold hard faces gave little away when I asked how he died. "Killed in the course of duty" was all they would say. Everything else was 'classified'.

They handed me a letter from my brother, saluted, then turned and left. I stood frozen to the spot, dazed, confused and devastated. I could not bear the loss of my brother. Finally, I opened the letter with trembling fingers but it only stared back at me. "I'll always be with you brother, John." What did he mean? How could he be with me ever again? He was dead.

Now, I leaned heavily on the dusty shovel in my hands and started to dig, determined to uncover the truth. The scar-faced man beside me began to dig at the other end of the grave and soon my brother's coffin began to emerge from beneath the layers of sodden Earth. Faced with this moment of truth, I began to panic.

What if I was wrong? I knew John hated the army; I knew he wanted to be out. I looked down at the coffin as my hired helper tugged at the lid with a crowbar. With a loud snap, the lid flew back revealing the frozen corpse inside. My whole body was filled with relief when I saw that the dead man in the coffin was not my brother.

(ii)

For the Motion

An old age home or a senior citizen home is a multi-residence housing facility intended solely for the elderly. Additional facilities are provided within the building like meals, gatherings, recreational activities and some form of health care. A place in a retirement home can be paid for on a rental basis. Most of the residents of such homes are kept there by their children as the children feel that the parents will be a burden on them. However, parents can never find mental peace in such a home as their family members are not present there.

Further, we must look after our parents in their declining years, just as they had cared for us in our formative years. They faithfully carried out their duty at that time. When they are no longer able to manage themselves, we must fulfil our duty and take care of them. They have spent most of their lifetime for us. So, it is our responsibility to care for them now. We have achieved difficult goals in our lives only due to their support. If they hadn't spent their time and money on us when we needed it, we wouldn't have been enjoying a comfortable life now. In addition, by caring for them now, we can set an example for our children so that when we grow old and helpless, our children will take care of us.

So, our parents should stay with us, if they desire, till they pass away. I am opposed to leaving our parents in an old age home because they will not find any mental peace there. I request everybody not to send their parents in old age homes. Even if they get proper attention and medical treatment there, they will not get the company of their children or grandchildren which they get in their houses. Once we stop sending our elderly family members to such homes, they will no longer be necessary.

Against the Motion

In today's world, old age homes are necessary, especially in India. Parents educate their children but, when children find work, get married and start a family, they may settle down in a different city or even a different country. The new location may not suit their parents as they are used to living in their hometowns. Hence, if someone looks after their needs at the place where they stay, it is well and good.

At present, the world is progressing very fast and the new generation is not necessarily tied down to one place for a lifetime. When they shift, parents may not go with them as the climate may not be suitable for them or the new home may be smaller or there may be other problems. In such a situation, their children are ready to pay for their welfare. This makes the availability of old age homes necessary as these homes fulfill several needs of elderly people.

Such homes provide assistance in several areas including security, financial, physical and medical needs. Some people are too busy due to various reasons. They think they will not be able to care for the elderly and, thus, they find it better to send them to old age homes. Other adults are financially not well-off so looking after the elderly in their family becomes improbable for them. Even if they wish to, it is difficult for them to look after their parents. In any of these cases, the children have the choice to send their parents to old age homes.

Thus, these homes play an important role. If the elders are kept there, they will get regular medical check-ups and have a time of their own. They can play games which do not require much physical exertion, indulge in their hobbies, interact and relax. They will feel happy when their children occasionally visit them. The children also feel happy that their parents are being looked after. Thus, old age homes are absolutely necessary.

(iii) **An Embarrassing Day in My Life**

The proverb 'Pride comes before a fall' became very apt for me. I was also good in academics and managed to come in the first three ranks in the class with the minimum of effort. The result was that I became egotistic and started making fun of my classmates especially because some of my class fellows laughed at my witticism. My grades encouraged me further and I started misbehaving when some lenient teachers were present.

One day, when the Hindi period started, our teacher walked into the class just as the bell rang. I had just sat down when the previous teacher had left and I did not notice our Hindi teacher coming in. All the children around me stood up and wished her. I was still sitting and, before I could get up, she saw me seated and thought that I was trying to insult her. As a punishment she made me stand the whole period on the chair. The whole class kept looking at me whispering and laughing. Instead of stopping the children, she asked me how I felt to be at the receiving end for once. I had never felt so humiliated in my life. On the top of it, she pointed out at my hairstyle and compared it to the one we see in the promotional advertisement for the candy 'Centre Shock'.

Everyone bursts into peals of laughter. I felt ashamed and realised how other children felt when I ridiculed them. Thankfully, I was made to sit down in the next period. No one was in a mood to study as it was the last period of the day. One of my friends imitated the way our Sanskrit teacher spoke but in a very exaggerated manner. I could not help and burst out laughing.

My teacher got so furious at me that she lost her temper and took me to the Principal's office. There, I stood outside the office for almost twenty minutes. To add to my embarrassment, there was a football tournament in our school that day.

Children from other schools were also participating. One of them happened to be my neighbour with whom I never got along. When he passed by me and snickered, I wished the Earth to crack and swallow me up.

What an embarrassing day! I shall never forget it. I resolved that I would never behave like that ever again.

(iv) A month ago, I moved to the USA to join the Masters Programme in Education at the Johns Hopkins University in the city of Baltimore. I couldn't get any accommodation in the University but I managed to find a place to stay in the neighbouring Charles Village.

It took me almost a month to settle down as I missed my home back in Mumbai. But, as I got used to life in the US, I realised that a lot of differences existed between Mumbai and Baltimore although both are densely populated.

I saw people rushing to work and students to college just as in Mumbai. However, I noticed that the Mumbai residents were always rushing; but still it took a long time commuting every day. But, here in Baltimore, I don't have to worry about how I am going to reach my college. There are shuttle services from Charles Village to the University.

Further, I had read and heard about how one can enjoy life in Mumbai but I never managed to make my way past crowded trains and chaotic streets. I tried eating street food at night on Abdul Rehman Street as I had heard about the delicious food served there.

The place, however, was so crowded and unhygienic that I literally turned back and went home. On the other hand, in Baltimore, street food is served in places that don't suffocate you with nausea and heat. I love going to the Paper Moon Diner or Jong Kak, both of which have wonderful menus.

Another difference which I have noticed is people's behaviour in public places. At the Taraporewala Aquarium in Mumbai, the visitors were unruly. I saw teenagers hitting the glass of the tanks, shouting and laughing out loud, and not paying attention to the aquarium guide. When last weekend, I went to the National Aquarium in Baltimore, no such unruly visitors were there. In fact, it was all very quiet.

Thus, I have realised that even the fast-paced life here in Baltimore is organised and people have proper etiquette. People do rush to work and colleges but they also find time to engage in recreational activities. And, when they do that, they do not cause inconvenience to others.

(v) **Rainwater Harvesting**

The given picture mentions rainwater harvesting which is one of the most effective methods of water conservation. In a developing country like India where there is a huge gap in demand and supply of fresh water, this method can be very useful. Water is an important element of human life and, as fresh water is getting scarcer, the need for water harvesting is increasing. In India, we get most of the water supply from rivers and lakes.

As the local footprints dry out due to mismanagement and overuse, the search for another resource turns even more distant, the situation takes an ironical turn. On one hand, the cities are facing severe water crisis and, on the other hand, they are flooded with rainwater which is the most common source of freshwater in monsoon. Today, the hunt for a water source and its sustainability is a big concern. One of the solutions for water crisis is collecting this abundant rainwater through rainwater harvesting.

This method aims to collect and store rainwater for use by humans, animals, in agriculture and in industries. In this process, rainwater is collected on roofs, parks and roads before it runs off. It is redirected to a tank, pit, cistern or reservoir and collected there.

Benefits of rainwater harvesting are as follows

- The cost incurred to recharge the groundwater is lower than maintaining surface reserves.
- The land is not occupied for storage purpose nor does the population needs to be moved from one place to another.
- Groundwater has minimum scope for evaporation or pollution which means more reliable for daily consumption.
- Rainwater harvesting and groundwater recharge also minimises the chance of flood like situations and consumption. Also, soil erosion can be checked with water harvesting.

2. (i) 79, Sector 4, RK Puram,
New Delhi-110045

12th August, 20XX

The Director,
Elite School of Language,
South Extension-II,
New Delhi-110048
Subject Enquiry regarding a course in communication skills
Dear Sir/Ma'am,
This letter is in reference to your advertisement in 'The Times of India' dated 10th August, 20XX in which there was an announcement about the new course in Communication Skills that you have introduced. I have passed Class XII and plan to take up a part-time job as a Customer Care Executive in a reputed call centre.
For this, I shall need to improve my communication skills and would appreciate it if you could forward me the details of the course.
Please let me know the duration of the course for beginners and the advanced course as well as the fees charged for both courses. I would like to know if they are diploma or certificate courses and also timings of the classes. Kindly provide the details to the address mentioned above as early as possible so that I can decide about enrolling myself for one of them.
Thanking you,
Yours sincerely,
Rajat Kumar

(ii) B-Bharat Vihar,
Kolkata

17th July, 20XX

Dear Suresh,
I am upset to hear that you have lost your job at the Institute of Technology. Did you know it was coming or was it very sudden? I remember you were quite happy and excited about the prospect of working in that company.
I hope that this change, while an upsetting one, will turn out to be a blessing in disguise. Bear with this difficult time and you will certainly come through a better opportunity. Wish you a good luck in finding a new job.
Remember, you are my closest friend. Please let me know if I can help you in any way possible.
Don't lose hope and take good care of yourself beside hunting for new jobs
Yours lovingly,
Aditya

3. (i)

ACT! ACTING! ACTION!

Inter-House Dramatics Competition
On 11th January, 20XX
from 11:00 a.m. to 4:00 p.m.
in the Auditorium, VPS, Hyderabad
All the House Captains must submit the scripts of the play being enacted by their House to the Cultural Secretary by 5th January, 20XX.

(ii) **To** principal@vps.org
Subject Prize to be Awarded in Inter-House Dramatics Competition
Dear Sir/Ma'am,
This is to inform you that all the students have been notified about the Inter-House Dramatics Competition to be held on 11th January, 20XX. I further request you to make a decision regarding the prize to be awarded to the winners and the certificates that will be awarded to the participants.
Kindly let me know as soon as possible so that I can move forward accordingly.
Thanking you,

Yours obediently,
Vandita Ghoshal
Cultural Secretary

4. (i) (1) (b) threw
(2) (d) Both (a) and (c)
(ii) (b) accidentally
(iii) (a) The author says that he is an Indian by accident because he has many identities because of his connection with many cultures within India.
(b) The author's desire 'to change the world' (which he then thought he could) brought him to what was then known as Bombay.
(c) The quality in himself that the author attributes to his Bengali DNA is protesting against happenings that do not concern him in the least.
(d) The author seems to have the similarity with Nirad C Chaudhuri of being a migrant in his own land who is trying to discover himself through his many identities.
(e) The passing Jesuit on the road took pity on the author's family when they were wandering on the roads and gave them shelter in Bishnupur where he ran a school.
(iv) The author discovers the magic of being Indian after wandering through his many identities. These include his regional culture, the languages he speaks, the faith he follows and the state to which he belongs. He discovers this by accident after going through the various identities, just like many other Indians.

5. (i) (1) lost (2) meeting (3) did not have (4) shot
(5) avoid (6) slammed (7) was destined (8) spun
(ii) (a) by (b) till (c) at (d) with
(e) in (f) by (g) during (h) by
(iii) (1) (c) Though the minister was wise, the king did not trust him.
(2) (b) When we reached the port, the storm came on.
(3) (b) One should neither borrow nor lend money.
(4) (d) She will win the prize as she deserves it.
(iv) (1) (c) I never listen to rap music.
(2) (a) The book doesn't belong to me.
(3) (a) The baby is not sleeping at the moment.
(4) (c) What do you think of this school?
(5) (c) I had left by the time they arrived.
(6) (b) Sam fell while playing football.
(7) (b) He will not be asked by them.
(8) (a) He said that they would be arriving there by the next train.

SQP Code : **PB-8/10** Series *i*-**Succeed 8-25/10** Roll No.

Sample Question Paper 08

English Language 10th (Code 01)

General Instructions

1. You will not be allowed to write during the first 15 minutes. This time is to be spent in reading the question paper.
2. The time given at the head of this paper is the time allowed for writing the answers.
3. Attempt all five questions.
4. The intended marks for questions or parts of questions are given in brackets [].
5. You are advised to spend not more than 30 minutes in answering Question 1 and 20 minutes in answering Question 2.

Time : 2 Hrs.

Max. Marks : 80

Question 1.

(Do not spend more than 30 minutes on this question.)

Write a composition (300-350 words) on **any one** of the following. [20]

(i) You went to the bank one morning for some work. While you were there, some robbers entered the bank to rob it but they were caught red-handed due to your presence of mind. Write an account of the robbery in your own words. Give it a suitable title.

(ii) "Technology has made us overly dependent on its existence." Express your views either for or against this statement.

(iii) You have been living in your ancestral home since birth. It is being acquired by the government because the Metro line has to pass through the area. Narrate the incident and describe your feelings about moving out of this house.

(iv) Write an original short story entitled 'A Silver Key'.

(v) Study the picture given below. Write a story or a description or an account of what it suggests to you. Your composition may be about the subject of the picture or you may take suggestions from it; however, there must be a clear connection between the picture and your composition.

Question 2.

(Do not spend more than 20 minutes on this question.)

Select **any one** of the following. [10]

(i) Write a letter to the Editor 'The Times of India' about evoking awareness for the use of solar energy among the citizens of India. You are Daman/Damini Yadav from Vijay Nagar, New Delhi.

(ii) You want to sell your cricket set. You think a friend of yours might like to buy it from you. Write a letter to your friend. In your letter, explain why you are selling the cricket set and the contents of the set. Also, suggest a date when your friend can come to see it.

Question 3.

(i) Recently, it was in the news that a hurricane hit the USA and around 13 states were affected. Being the Head Girl of your school, draft a notice for the students and staff appealing for donations of relief products like clothes, money, books and other articles. [5]

(ii) Write an email to the principal of the neighbouring school informing him of the event and requesting him to ask students for donations. You are Amrita Shastri, secretary of Vijay Public School. [5]

Question 4.

Read the following passage carefully and answer the questions that follow :

Using vague words and phrases such as 'you know,' 'nice' and 'interesting' too often in a speech does not make good sense. "That's an interesting comment"; "That's a nice presentation"; "It was a nice meeting" are expressions which don't convey much and sound apologetic at the same time. Try and use precise words so as to make an impact. Make an effort to choose the right word to describe your opinion. To be able to do that, you will need to work on your vocabulary. Reading is the best way to improve your vocabulary. Pay attention to any new word you come across and see how you can incorporate it in a sentence. Never use slang in office. Never get into the buddy mode in office. Reserve it for socialising. Effective communication comes in handy to soften bad news.

It is very painful to tell a subordinate that he/she is not required anymore. You wouldn't enjoy saying 'You're fired!' to anyone. Instead, say: "We're very sorry we have to let you go." It is less painful for the person. And, of course you have to do it in private perhaps in a conference room or a closed office cabin so that the person can express his/her emotions and be spared the agony of an **inquisitive** audience. A good sense of humour is an asset that strengthens communication skills. There are also occasions when one has to say 'no' to many things and many people. We all encounter people who soft-talk you by saying, "Please, could you do this for me?" Saying 'no' is not only rude but also can affect relationships. Instead, say, "I'd do it if only I had four more hands and two more heads." Don't say this rudely. Say it jovially with a smile so as to let the other person know you mean no offence but you simply cannot spare the time to do that job.

Always keep your language simple and don't **sprinkle** it with too many fancy words or jargon. Mispronunciations can badly affect your image. So, make an effort to pronounce words correctly. The sound of your voice is an important as the variety of your vocabulary. The best way to judge how you sound is by using a tape recorder. Read out a passage. Notice that the tone and pace of your voice changes each time.

Note the strengths and improvise on the weaknesses. Speaking well is a great confidence-booster.

You feel good if you sound good. And, keep working on your voice, vocabulary and pronunciation. Last, but not the least, one of the most important traits of an effective communicator is that he/she is also a good listener. Only if one learns to listen carefully can one respond appropriately. Be attentive, ask for clarifications when you don't understand, don't interrupt, note down points you wish to clarify and discuss them later.

Remember, there may be many good speakers, but one has to be a good listener to become an effective communicator.

(i) For each word given below, choose the correct meaning (as used in the passage) from the options provided. [2]

(1) *inquisitive* (line 14)
  (a) showing no interest in anything
  (b) eager to find things out
  (c) the quality of indifference
  (d) to be nonchalant about something

(2) *Sprinkle* (line 22)
  (a) powder (b) distribute (c) light rain (d) decorate

(ii) Which word in the passage means the opposite of the word 'exclude'? [1]
  (a) convey (b) incorporate (c) encounter (d) improvise

(iii) Answer the following questions briefly in your own words.
  (a) Suggest any two points to make your vocabulary rich. [2]
  (b) How does effective communication help you reduce the agony of a listener to whom the information may be painful? [2]
  (c) How does poor communication affect relationships? [2]
  (d) How does listening contribute to being an effective communicator? [2]
  (e) What role does humour play in communication? [1]

(iv) In not more than 50 words, describe what the author wants to convey about communication. [8]

Question 5.

(i) Fill in each of the numbered blanks with the correct form of the word given in brackets. Do not copy the passage but write in correct serial order the word or phrase appropriate to the blank space. [4]

Example

The car .....**(0)**..... (slow) down at the curve.

Answer : (0) slowed

Gandhiji ....**(1)** .... (be) a prolific writer who .... **(2)** .... (spend) several hours in a day writing. He .... **(3)** .... (write) for the journals that he then .... **(4)** .... (edit). He .... **(5)** .... (use) the print medium for .... **(6)** .... (spread) his message. His personal letters .... **(7)** .... (be) even more powerful. Thus, he .... **(8)** .... (apply) a powerful medium to reinforce his views on life.

(ii) Fill in the blanks with appropriate words. [4]
  (a) I commenced work .... the month of May.
  (b) We walked .... the street .... the end.
  (c) The child has been missing .... his home .... yesterday.
  (d) Ravi drove his car 180 m/s .... two hours .... stopping anywhere.
  (e) I received this message .... 7 o'clock .... the morning.
  (f) I saw Jagdish felling a big tree .... an axe.
  (g) An old feud existed .... the two families.
  (h) .... Anil and Vinod, there were three other boys present.

(iii) Join the following sentences to make one complete sentence **without using and, but** or **so**. Choose the correct option. [4]

(1) Mr. Sharma's heart attack was severe. He was bedridden for six months.
(a) Though Mr. Sharma was bedridden for six months, his heart attack was severe.
(b) Though Mr. Sharma's heart attack was severe, he was bedridden for six months.
(c) Mr. Sharma was bedridden for six months after a severe heart attack.
(d) Mr. Sharma's heart attack was severe after he was bedridden.

(2) Jagdish went out to see the damage due to the earthquake. Sarita stayed back to look after the baby.
(a) While Jagdish went out to see the damage due to the earthquake, Sarita stayed back to look after the baby.
(b) Jagdish went out to see the damage due to the earthquake because Sarita stayed back to look after the baby.
(c) Sarita stayed back to look after the baby; nonetheless, Jagdish went out to see the damage due to the earthquake.
(d) Jagdish went out to see the damage due to earthquake; moreover, Sarita stayed back to look after the baby.

(3) Ranee warned her daughter, Poonam, against talking to unknown persons. She told Poonam not to accept gifts from strangers.
(a) Ranee warned her daughter, Poonam, either to talk to strangers or to accept gifts from them.
(b) Ranee warned her daughter, Poonam, neither to talk to strangers nor to accept gifts from them.
(c) Ranee warned her daughter, Poonam, not only to not talk to strangers but also to accept gifts from them.
(d) Ranee warned her daughter, Poonam, to not talk to strangers yet to accept gifts from them.

(4) Everyone was drenched thoroughly. The rain was coming down in torrents.
(a) Everyone was drenched thoroughly yet the rain was coming down in torrents.
(b) The rain was coming down in torrents since everyone was drenched thoroughly.
(c) The rain was coming down in torrents; however, everyone was drenched thoroughly.
(d) Everyone was drenched thoroughly because the rain was coming down in torrents.

(iv) Choose the correct option to rewrite the following according to instructions given after each sentence. [8]

(1) This was the best drama I had ever enjoyed.
[Begin with : Never]
(a) This was the best drama I had never not enjoyed.
(b) This was the best drama I had never enjoyed.
(c) Never had I enjoyed a better drama than this.
(d) Never did I enjoyed a better drama than this.

SP-08

(2) Come what may, we will have the match tomorrow.
[Begin with : Whatever]
(a) Whatever may happen, we will have the match tomorrow.
(b) Whatever will happen, we will have the match tomorrow.
(c) Whatever could happen, we will have the match tomorrow.
(d) Whatever does happen, we will have the match tomorrow.

(3) Do your parents allow you to watch TV late at night?
[Rewrite using : let]
(a) Do your parents let you watch TV late at night?
(b) Do you let your parents watch TV late at night?
(c) Do your parents let TV watch late at night?
(d) None of the above

(4) I've never tasted such good food before.
[Rewrite using : ever]
(a) It's the best food I've ever tasted.
(b) Even it's the best food I've tasted.
(c) Never have I ever not tasted the best food.
(d) None of these

(5) It's not possible to play tennis because of the rain.
[Use : makes]
(a) The rain makes tennis impossible.
(b) The tennis game makes the rain impossible.
(c) The playing of tennis makes it impossible to rain.
(d) The rain makes it impossible to play tennis.

(6) I saw the film although I strongly dislike thrillers.
[Use : spite]
(a) I saw the film despite of my strong dislike of thrillers.
(b) I saw the film despite my strong liking of thrillers.
(c) I saw the film in spite my strong liking of thrillers.
(d) I saw the film in spite of my strong dislike of thrillers.

(7) The child disappeared as soon as the bus stopped.
[Begin : Hardly......]
(a) Hardly had the bus stopped that the child disappeared.
(b) Hardly had the bus stopped than the child disappeared.
(c) Hardly did the bus stop then the child disappeared.
(d) Hardly had the bus stopped when the child disappeared.

(8) She said, "I don't want to come with you."
[Begin with : She said that...]
(a) She said that she doesn't want to come with me.
(b) She said that she didn't want to come with me.
(c) She said that she didn't want to come with you.
(d) She said that she doesn't want to come with you.

Answers *in Topper's Style*

1. (i) **Bank Robbery Foiled**

Last week, I went to the bank as I had to get a Demand Draft (DD) made. After submitting my application for the DD, I sat down on a bench to wait. Suddenly, the front door of the bank opened and three men entered who did not appear to be normal customers. They were all wearing caps and dark glasses.

One of them was also carrying a big bag. I immediately became suspicious about their intentions.

The men barged into the branch manager's cabin and asked him to hand over the keys of the storage room where most of the cash was stored. One of the robbers took out a pistol from his pocket and threatened the manager. He also threatened other employees of the bank not to move from their place or he would kill them. I then realised that these men were robbers. The manager meekly handed over the storage room keys, and pleaded with the robber holding the pistol not to shoot. Two of the robbers snatched the keys and headed towards the storage room while the one with the pistol waved it around and shouted, "There are real bullets in this gun."

I had been a regular visitor to this bank as I had held an account here for the last 8 years. On one of my previous visits, I had accidentally seen the place where a secret alarm was installed. If pressed, it would alert the nearest police station which was about 500 metres away. I realised that as a responsible citizen it was my duty to help fight against crime. So, I quietly moved towards the corner of the room where the secret alarm button was. After looking to see where the robber with the pistol was, I pressed the alarm button firmly for sometime.

Soon, the two robbers came out of the storage room with the bag full of currency notes. As they reached the front door, the door burst open and two policemen brandishing hand guns rushed in. Thus, the robbers were caught red-handed. They gave in without a fight and were immediately handcuffed.

When the bank manager came to know that I had pressed the alarm button, he thanked me profusely.

I personally felt that I had only done my duty.

(ii) **For the Motion**

Billy Lox, a very famous American bassist said, "Technology should improve your life, not become your life." That's one thing that every one of us should learn and adopt. We need technology just to improve and help us do our work, which otherwise would be time consuming, in a much easier and faster way. That is it.

We do not have to become slaves of technology. Gadgets, equipments, machines etc. are just a part of life not a way of life. We need to loosen our grip on technology and tighten it on human interaction. Albert Einstein once said, "I fear the day that technology will surpass our human interaction. The world will have a generation of idiots." We definitely do not want our generation and the coming generations to be skill-less nitwits.

Gone are the days when kids would want to play outside in the parks or gardens. They now want to have a smart phone, laptop or a television in front of them where they can play games, watch shows, etc.
We know that these actions have serious repercussions.

Depression, insomnia, hyperactivity disorder which are some major disorders that today's kids are facing are directly linked to gadgets. A very important question here is not what technology has done and is doing 'for' us but what technology has done and is doing 'to' us. One-to-one communication is losing its essence.

While sitting together for dinner in a restaurant, in a party, in a family gathering or any social event, people are seen glued to their smart phone. Reading stories to children, listening to live music, having a soulful conversation with a family member or friend seem like forgotten tales.

Our increasing dependence on technology for getting us through all our daily chores, our day-to-day obligatory communication, our days and our nights, is removing the power of choice. We take what technology has to offer without weighing our options because it's easy and quick that way. I conclude with the proverb—'Technology is a useful servant but a very, very dangerous master.'

Against the Motion

American Physicist Freeman Dyson said, "Technology is a gift of God. After the gift of life, it is perhaps the greatest of God's gifts. It is the mother of civilisations, of arts and of sciences." Technology has given us the freedom to express ourselves in an open forum. It has given us the opportunity to see the things we had only dreamt of. It is present in every aspect of our lives enriching us and our work's output.

I agree that too much dependency on technology is not called for. But, right from morning till the end of our day, we have to use technology for something or the other, be it making a smoothie for breakfast or using an elevator to get to the 25th floor or to present an impressionable PowerPoint presentation, technology is omnipresent.

The field of health and medicine would still be reeling under manual scans, the authentication of which was always doubtful. Enter hi-tech technology, the scene changes. Accurate diagnosis, surgical procedures, improved patient care, etc. are the result of development of some brilliant medical innovations like MRI machines, artificial organs and robotic prosthetic limbs.

Technology is the best when it brings people together. So many of us have reconnected with friends and acquaintances that we had not seen or heard from in years. Social media is a very precious gift from technology to us. Our world has come closer. Inter personal communication is better, faster and, most of all, possible.

Sending money, gifts and consignments anywhere in the world was a nearly impossible dream. Even if it was possible, it was either very time-consuming or expensive. Now, we can do all these things with a snap of our fingers. No boundaries separate nations. We all are on one global platform.

Technology has given the word 'possibility' a new and wider dimension. We can hope and imagine better and easier ways of living our lives. We are changing the world with it. Technology will never replace great thinkers but, in the hands of great thinkers, it is transformational. It is used every day in every field in everything we do.

(iii) My grandfather came to Delhi as a refugee from what had just been named Pakistan in 1947 with his parents. In return for the land that he had left behind, he had been allotted some land in what was now the capital of the independent India–New Delhi. On this land, over the span of four years, he gradually built a lovely new house. Until last week, it was the only home I had ever known but now it is to be demolished.

Over the last few years, sweeping changes have taken place in Delhi; with the advent of the Metro, the geography of the city is being altered. Suddenly, it has become possible to go from one end of the city to the other in just over an hour and that too in air-conditioned comfort. As time goes by, the Metro is going to expand. It will soon cut through entirely new localities and neighbourhoods as it makes it easier than ever before to get to different places in the city.

Unfortunately, our house happened to be right in the path of a new line of the Delhi Metro. Thus, the house had to go. The government bought it from us for a princely sum and while this allowed us to buy another house, it could do nothing to alleviate the pain we felt at shifting out of a house that the family had lived in for over 70 years.

As we packed our belongings and began moving our luggage out, each of us was crying.

Four generations of my family had lived in this house, and it was suffused with the memories of all the time we had spent here. I myself had grown up in its various rooms, corridors and gardens, and was heart-broken at the thought that very soon it would cease to even exist. Still, a new house meant new rooms and a new neighbourhood to explore, and that was a heartening thought for the time being.

(iv) **A Silver Key**

It was a very stormy night with the wind howling and the rain falling incessantly. A traveller had got down at the town's bus stand and was looking for a place to stay. Then, he saw the signboard of a *dharmshala* just a few yards down the road so he went there to seek shelter.

He was highly disappointed to find the door locked from inside. However, he could see a light shining inside through a closed window. So, he knocked loudly on the door.

Someone, who the traveller assumed was the keeper of the *dharmshala*, called out from inside, "I am sorry; I am unable to open the door because I have lost the key."

The traveller replied, "But, I want to stay the night here. I am totally soaked due to the rain. Please allow me to come inside."

The keeper replied, "I'm sorry but the door can only be unlocked with a silver key. Do you have a silver key?"

The traveller, who was quite intelligent, understood what was wanted of him. He put his hand inside his pocket and brought out a silver one rupee coin. He pushed this coin under the front door. Sure enough, it brought the desired result. Soon, the front door opened and the traveller was allowed to enter.

The *dharmshala* keeper was standing at the door with a smug smile on his face. He said, "Welcome to the only *dharmshala* in this town."

As soon as the traveller got inside, he thanked the keeper and requested him to bring in his suitcase.

The keeper went outside to get it. As soon as the keeper stepped outside, the traveller shut the door and locked it. The keeper shouted from outside, "What kind of joke is this? Open the door immediately!"

"It is not a joke", answered the traveller.

"I am sorry, I have lost the key. The door can be opened only with a silver key."

The keeper had to push the silver coin under the door. The traveller, only after getting his rupee back, let the dishonest man in.

(v) **A Cruise at Sea Goes Wrong**

The given picture shows a ship sinking in the sea. This is a real incident which I encountered when my family decided to take a holiday by cruising around the Mediterranean Sea to know more about Europe at a leisurely pace. The cruise ship MV Sharda had started from Rome carrying over 400 passengers around the islands in the Mediterranean Sea for a 10-day trip. As it was my first time on a cruise ship, I was rather apprehensive about falling seasick.

However, my parents said that I would get used to sea soon enough and would enjoy the trip. In addition, I would learn a lot about European history and visit some of the historic places which I had so far seen only in History books. We absorbed much of history and culture with each passing day of our trip. On the 7th day of the trip, we docked at the port of Aegina. It was a warm and sunny day; we were eating lunch in a restaurant on the upper deck. I finished my pudding and went to the bridge of the ship to look around.

Suddenly, I heard loud screams and there was a violent jerk such that I lost my balance and fell hitting my head on the deck. It appeared as if something heavy had struck the ship. Soon, the ship started to tilt and go down. I was suddenly reminded of a similar scene in the movie 'Titanic'. So, I quickly stood up and went down to the restaurant just below.

The door was jammed and I had to kick it open. Everything was in a mess; some tables had fallen down and water was streaming in. Suddenly, I heard the captain's voice shouting for everyone to evacuate the ship immediately. Luckily, as we were docked, we could climb out on the jetty where we were berthed.

Just as we disembarked, we saw the ship was already half inside the water. It appeared that another ship coming into the harbour had hit our ship on the side. What a narrow escape we had! I felt happy that all the passengers had survived although we lost most of our luggage.

2. (i) B1/139, Vijay Nagar,
Khureji Khas,
New Delhi-110051

29th March, 20XX

The Editor,
The Times of India,
New Delhi-110002

Subject Raising awareness regarding the use of solar energy

Respected Sir/Ma'am,

Through the columns of your esteemed newspaper, I wish to make people aware of the growing need for the use of solar power. We all know that the Earth is showing signs of declining health. It is excessive pollution and excessive use of resources, particularly fossil fuels, that is leading to this situation. Man has a desire to lead a luxurious life and for that he is overusing the resources.

To find alternate sources of energy, we should switch over to the use of solar energy through solar cookers, solar lanterns, solar water heaters and solar electric panels. All these items are available in the market and the government should subsidise them so that more and more people switch over to this option.

I am sure that, by using alternate energy, we will be able to cut down the pollution level and make Earth a better place to live in.

Thanking you,

Yours sincerely,
Damini Yadav

(ii) 145, Neel Kamal Colony,
New Delhi -110002

5th August, 20XX

Dear Gaurav,

We haven't met for some time but I am hoping that you are doing well. My life has become a little hectic at the moment as my father has got an assignment abroad and we will be moving there soon. There is so much to do!

There are a few things that I can't take with me so I am seeing if any of my friends would be interested in buying them. One of the things I do not want to take with me is my cricket set and I thought you might like to buy it off me for a cheap price.

The set has a full size bat which is made of the finest willow wood. It comes with a set of wickets, helmet, pads and gloves. You know my habit of keeping my things well; so, everything in the cricket set is in very good condition.

I'm leaving the country at the end of the month which is only two weeks away. So, if you want to see it, it would be best to come on 20th or 21st. That will give me time to sell it elsewhere if you are not interested.

I look forward to seeing you. Let me know if you can't make it.

All the best

Yours truly,
Manish

3. (i)

Appeal for Donations

8th December, 20XX
from 9 : 00 am to 4 : 00 pm
at Skating Ring, Vijay Public School

Our Students Council has organised a rehabilitation drive for the victims of the recent hurricane in the United States of America. One can donate clothes, books, articles like blanket, blazer, quilt, etc. Certificates will be given to the major contributors. For further queries, contact the head girl.

(ii) **To** principal.sas@gmail.com

Subject Request to send donations for the Rehabilitation Drive

Dear Sir/Ma'am,

The school is going to organise a rehabilitation drive for the victims of the recent hurricane in the USA on 8th December from 9 : 00 am to 4 : 00 pm in the school auditorium. Kindly ask students from your school to participate in this event and donate useful items. It is important to prove our humanity during these tough times. Please explain to your students the purpose of this drive and help us make this effort a success.

Thanking you

Yours faithfully,

Amrita Shastri

Secretary

Vijay Public School

4. (i) (1) (b) eager to find things out (2) (b) distribute

(ii) (b) incorporate

(iii) (a) A good vocabulary helps in carrying out good communication. Vocabulary can be made rich by reading books and newspapers. One should also make a note of any new word that one comes across and try to use it in a sentence.

(b) Communication of some information that may be painful for the listener should be done in such a way that makes it easier for the listener to accept. This will help reduce the agony of the listener. For instance, if we have to terminate somebody's employment, reframing the communication can really console the listener.

(c) Poor communication affects relationships as we are unable to convey our true intentions properly or we are too blunt and offensive to the other person. In such a difficult situation, it is important not to be rude and to adopt a positive tone to speak our thoughts clearly as it can certainly save one's relationship.

(d) It is important to be a good listener to achieve expertise in effective communication. Listening is of prime importance because only then can we respond appropriately. We should listen carefully by understanding each and every word before responding. This results in good communication.

(e) Humour helps in alleviating a difficult situation. It helps in conveying our thoughts without being offensive and it also simplifies communication.

(iv) The author wants to convey the importance of communication in each and every aspect of our life, e.g. in the office where we refuse job to someone, or at home where true intentions need to be conveyed amicably. Being polite, using good vocabulary, adding humour and, most importantly, being a good listener helps in becoming a good communicator.

5. (i) (1) was (2) spent (3) wrote (4) edited

(5) used (6) spreading (7) were (8) applied

(ii) (a) from (b) down, to (c) from, since (d) within, without

(e) at, in (f) with (g) between (h) Besides

(iii) (1) (c) Mr. Sharma was bedridden for six months after a severe heart attack.

(2) (a) While Jagdish went out to see the damage due to the earthquake, Sarita stayed back to look after the baby.

(3) (b) Ranee warned her daughter, Poonam, neither to talk to strangers nor to accept gifts from them.

(4) (d) Everyone was drenched thoroughly because the rain was coming down in torrents.

(iv) (1) (c) Never had I enjoyed a better drama than this.

(2) (a) Whatever may happen, we will have the match tomorrow.

(3) (a) Do your parents let you watch TV late at night?

(4) (a) It is the best food I've ever tasted.

(5) (d) The rain makes it impossible to play tennis.

(6) (d) I saw the film in spite of my strong dislike of thrillers.

(7) (d) Hardly had the bus stopped when the child disappeared.

(8) (b) She said that she didn't want to come with me.

SQP Code : **PB-9/10** Series ***i*-Succeed 9-25/10** Roll No.

Sample Question Paper 09

English Language 10th (Code 01)

General Instructions

1. You will not be allowed to write during the first 15 minutes. This time is to be spent in reading the question paper.
2. The time given at the head of this paper is the time allowed for writing the answers.
3. Attempt all five questions.
4. The intended marks for questions or parts of questions are given in brackets [].
5. You are advised to spend not more than 30 minutes in answering Question 1 and 20 minutes in answering Question 2.

Time : 2 Hrs.

Max. Marks : 80

Question 1.

(Do not spend more than 30 minutes on this question.)

Write a composition (300-350 words) on **any one** of the following. [20]

(i) Write an original short story starting with the words 'If only I had told the truth ....'

(ii) 'Brain drain is adversely affecting India's development.'
Express your views for or against this statement.

(iii) Your house is near a river. Everyday, you see people using sail boats to go across or riding for fun. You got an opportunity to learn how to sail using a sail boat. Narrate your experience.

(iv) During summer holidays, your family had planned to visit your grandfather's place which is in Himachal Pradesh. Your father decided to travel by road in his own car. Describe the journey and your experience during it.

(v) Study the picture given below. Write a story or a description or an account of what the picture suggests to you. Your composition may be about the subject of the picture or you may take suggestions from it but there must be a clear connection between the picture and your composition.

Question 2.

(Do not spend more than 20 minutes on it.)

Select **any one** of the following. [10]

(i) Write a letter to the Director of the Archaeological Survey of India complaining about the damage caused to a historical monument in your city due to negligence.

(ii) You are Ananya/Anand. Write a letter to your sister describing your new boarding school and the facilities it provides you.

Question 3.

(i) Ira is the Head Girl of Vanasthali Public School, Ludhiana. She has lost her hall ticket for the Board Examination. She puts up a notice on the school notice board. Draft the notice to help her find the ticket. [5]

(ii) You are Mr. Deepak, the Librarian of KVAFA. Write an e-mail to Ira informing her that you have found her hall ticket for the Board Examination. [5]

Question 4.

Read the following passage carefully and answer the questions that follows.

Ashfaqullah Khan was a loyal friend, a great revolutionary ; a real martyr who sacrificed his life for the cause of freedom. By his unique sacrifice, Ashfaqulla Khan became an **immortal** revolutionary an unforgettable name in the Indian freedom struggle history. Born in Shahjahanpur, Uttar Pradesh, Ashfaqulla Khan was the son of Sahfiqulla Khan. In 1921, Mahatma Gandhi had called on all Indians not to pay taxes to the government or cooperate with the British. This non-cooperation movement **kindled** the fire of freedom in the hearts of all Indians. However, with the Chauri Chaura violence which resulted in the setting ablaze of a police station and death of some policemen, Mahatma Gandhi called off the non-cooperation movement in February 1922. The youth of the country were greatly disappointed with this calling off of the movement and they themselves resolved that the country should become free as early as possible. Ashfaqulla Khan joined the band of such revolutionaries. Ramprasad Bismil, who also hailed from Shahjahanpur, was the leader of the militant group of these revolutionaries. A friendship was cultivated between Ashfaqulla Khan and Ramprasad Bismil. He was an *Aryasamaji* whereas Ashfaqulla Khan was a devout Muslim. They were so devoted to the cause of the nation that their religion did not come in the way of their firm resolve to join together for the freedom struggle. Their friendship was so strongly fastened that they always moved together, ate together and worked together. They were called two bodied but one soul. An incident in this connection is worth mentioning. Once Ashfaq had severe fever and due to the very high temperature he was muttering Ram, my dear Ram. Ashfaq's parents became much perturbed and though that Ashfaq had been overpowered by some evil spirit since he was uttering the name of Ram, the Lord of Hindus. They called their neighbour. The neighbour reassured them, explaining that Ashfaq was remembering Ramprasad Bismil, his friend, whom he was in the habit of addressing as Ram Prasad Bismil was called Ashfaq's muttering came to a stop and both embraced each other.
They formed the Hindustan Republican Association. Shachindra Nath Sanyal was the founder of this organisation. Their objective was to win freedom for the country through armed revolution.

The association published a manifesto called Krantikari in 1925, advocating the elimination of inequality and slavery. For the purpose of carrying out the revolution, they needed money. The famous Kakori train robbery was conceived with the sole objective of getting money for carrying out their revolutionary activities. The train robbery was conceived by Ramprasad. Once while travelling from Shahjahanpur to Lucknow, he noticed money bags being taken into the guard's van and dropped into an iron safe. Ashfaq opposed the idea saying that it would be a hasty step and would expose the revolutionaries to direct attack by a strong government which would use its entire machinery to crush revolutionary activities. However, the revolutionaries decided to go ahead with the plan. Like a disciplined solider, Ashfaq vowed to join in it.

(i) For each word given below, choose the correct meaning (as used in the passage) from the options provided : [2]

(1) *immortal* (line 2)

(a) to be ephemeral (b) something that can be easily forgotten
(c) deserving to be remembered forever (d) something that is obscured

(2) *kindled* (line 6)

(a) mitigated (b) aroused (c) doused (d) ruined

(ii) Which word in the passage means the opposite of the word 'composed'? [1]

(a) overpowered (b) revolutionary (c) perturbed (d) disciplined

(iii) Answer the following questions briefly in your own words.

(a) Who called the Indians for the Non-cooperation Movement? How was it to be carried out? [2]

(b) Why was the Non-cooperation Movement called off? [2]

(c) What epithet did the friendship of Ashfaq and Ramprasad win them? [2]

(d) What plan was proposed by Ramprasad Bismil in order to materialise the mission of the revolution? [2]

(e) Why were Ashfaq's parents perturbed? [1]

(iv) Describe the character and life events of Ashfaqulla Khan based on the passage in your own words. Do not exceed 50 words. [8]

Question 5.

(i) Fill in each of the numbered blanks with correct form of the words given in brackets. Do not copy the passage but write in correct serial order the word of phrase appropriate to the blank space. [4]

Example He ....(0)......... (look) at his sister doubtfully.

Answer (0) looked

A few of my friends and I decided to visit Cherating during our school vacation. We knew that we were most certainly going to ......**(1)**...... (have) a good time.

It ......**(2)**...... (take) about one hour for us to ......**(3)**...... (drive) from Kuantan to Cherating. When we reached the place, we ......**(4)**...... (see) many fishing villages and beautiful beaches ......**(5)**...... (stretch) up to several kilometres. Cherating is sunny throughout the year and many people ......**(6)**...... (come) to Cherating either to swim or ......**(7)**...... (dive). While at Cherating, we also ......**(8)** ...... (enjoy) the excellent local food. Cherating is indeed one of Malaysia's best tourist attractions.

(ii) Fill in the blank with appropriate words. [4]

(a) He was shot .... a pistol.

(b) Someone came to meet you .... you were out.

(c) We watched TV .... two hours.

(d) .... his visit, the Pope will also bless the new hospital.

(e) I lived .... London for two years.

(f) I prefer watching sport events .... television to seeing them live in the stadium.

(g) I'll be at home .... the weekend. We can meet then.

(h) If you want to get books at a discount, get them .... 5th April, the last date of the book fair.

(iii) Join the following sentences to make one complete sentence **without using and, but** or **so**. Chooose the correct option. [4]

(1) He fell into bad habits. He became poor.
- (a) He became poor because he fell into bad habits.
- (b) He fell into bad habits and became poor.
- (c) He fell into bad habits while he became poor.
- (d) He became poor though he fell into bad habits.

(2) We could not buy anything. The market was closed.
- (a) We could not buy anything while the market was closed.
- (b) We could not buy anything whenever the market was closed.
- (c) We could not buy anything since the market was closed.
- (d) We could not buy anything otherwise the market was closed.

(3) The deer runs fast. The tiger runs faster.
- (a) The deer runs faster than the tiger.
- (b) The tiger does not run faster than the deer.
- (c) The deer does run faster than the tiger.
- (d) The tiger runs faster than the deer.

(4) She is ill. I must help her.
- (a) Because I must help her, she is ill.
- (b) As she is ill, I must help her.
- (c) Though she is ill, I must help her.
- (d) I must help her even if she is ill.

(iv) Choose the correct option to rewrite the following according to the instructions given after each sentence. [8]

(1) Sneha went to sleep after she had completed her homework.
[Begin with : When]
- (a) When Sneha completed her home work, she went to sleep.
- (b) When Sneha had completed her home work, she went to sleep.
- (c) When Sneha went to sleep, she had completed her home work.
- (d) None of the above

(2) Her grandmother is illiterate but still she has great understanding of education.
[Begin with : Despite]
- (a) Despite of being illiterate, her grandmother has great understanding of education.
- (b) Despite illiterated, her grandmother has great understanding of education.
- (c) Despite being illiterate, her grandmother has great understanding of education.
- (d) Despite she is illiterate, her grandmother has great understanding of education.

(3) Sonu Nigam was requested to sing a song.
[Rewrite using direct speech]
- (a) The audience said to Sonu Nigam, "Please, sing a song for us."
- (b) The audience said to Sonu Nigam, "Sing a song for us."
- (c) The audience said to Sonu Nigam, "Maybe sing a song for us?"
- (d) The audience said to Sonu Nigam, "Don't sing a song for us."

(4) The young generation prefers using electronic gadgets to playing games and sports.
[Begin with 'The young generation would rather…']

(a) The young generation would rather use electronic gadgets than play games and sports.
(b) The young generation would rather use games and sports than play electronic gadgets.
(c) The young generation would rather play games and sports than use electronic gadgets.
(d) All of the above

(5) Every human being has some flaw.
[Begin with : There]

(a) There is every human being who doesn't have a flaw.
(b) There is every human being who has a flaw.
(c) There is no human being who has a flaw.
(d) There is no human being who doesn't have a flaw.

(6) Pakistan has never faced a more humiliating defeat than this at the World Cup.
[End with : ever faced]

(a) This is not the most humiliating defeat at the World Cup that Pakistan has ever faced.
(b) This is probably the most humiliating defeat at the World Cup that Pakistan has ever faced.
(c) This is the most humiliating defeat at the World Cup that Pakistan has ever faced.
(d) None of the above

(7) He is too big a liar to be trusted by anyone.
[Rewrite using : so ... that]

(a) He is so big a liar that everyone can trust him.
(b) He is so big a liar that no one can trust him.
(c) He is so big a liar that everyone should trust him.
(d) He is so big a liar that no one should not trust him.

(8) Was she reading these lines?
[Rewrite using passive voice]

(a) Were these lines read by her?
(b) Were those lines read by her?
(c) Were those lines being by her read?
(d) Were these lines being read by her?

For Answers scan QR code

SQP Code : **PB-10/10** Series ***i*-Succeed 10-25/10** Roll No.

Sample Question Paper 10

English Language 10th (Code 01)

General Instructions

1. You will not be allowed to write during the first 15 minutes. This time is to be spent in reading the question paper.
2. The time given at the head of this paper is the time allowed for writing the answers.
3. Attempt all five questions.
4. The intended marks for questions or parts of questions are given in brackets [].
5. You are advised to spend not more than 30 minutes in answering Question 1 and 20 minutes in answering Question 2.

Time : 2 Hrs.

Max. Marks : 80

Question 1.

(Do not spend more than 30 minutes on this question.)

Write a composition (300-350 words) on **any one** of the following. [20]

(i) Write an original short story entitled 'Every cloud has a silver lining.'

(ii) Express your views either for or against the motion "Crime-based serials on TV lead to a reduction in crime".

(iii) You live in small city; recently, a mall has come up in your town. You visited this shopping mall along with your family for the first time in your life. Narrate your experience and mention what all you saw there and how you felt after visiting.

(iv) It is a matter of concern that there has been increase in deaths and accidents which are caused due to the endemic disorder called Road rage. People are showing great intolerance and there is total lack of self-discipline. Write composition on the topic 'Road Rage'.

(v) Study the picture given below. Write a story or a description or an account of what it suggests to you. Your composition may be about the subject of the picture or you may take suggestions from it; however, there must be a clear connection between the picture and your composition.

Question 2.

(Do not spend more than 20 minutes on it.)

Select **any one** of the following. [10]

(i) You are Binod/Bhawna Talwar, Warden of the hostel in Karuna Public School, Allahabad. Write an enquiry letter to the Marketing Manager, Prayag Domestic Appliances, Naini requesting a quotation for ceiling fans, tube light fixtures and other electric items required for the hostel. Specify the number required of each item and request for credit in the terms of payment.

(ii) Write a letter to your colleague, Mr. Raghavana apologising for misunderstanding of an act of generosity by him. You are R. Kumaraswami.

Question 3.

(i) You are Cultural Secretary of Queen Mary Convent, Lucknow. You want suitable students to represent your school in the Inter-School English Debate Competition to be held shortly. Providing the necessary details and write a notice inviting participation. [5]

(ii) Write an e-mail to an event organiser having mail id: nat_events@hotmail.com to enquire about purchase of decor for the Debate competition. Assume yourself to be Sunita Jalan. [5]

Question 4.

Read the following passage carefully and answer the questions that follow.

In Varanasi district, there is a village called Bira in which an old, childless widow used to live. She was a gond woman named Bhungi and she didn't own either a scrap of land or a house to live in. Her only source of livelihood was a parching oven. The village folk customarily have one meal a day of parched grains, so there was always a crowd around Bhungi's oven. Whatever grain she was paid for parching, she would grind or fry and eat it.
She slept in a corner of the same little shack that sheltered the oven. As soon as it was light she'd get up and go out to gather dry leaves from all around to make her fire. She would stack the leaves right next to the oven, and after twelve, light the fire. But on the days when she had to parch grain for Pandit Udaybhan Pandye, the owner of the village, she went to bed hungry.

She was obliged to work without pay for Pandit Udaybhan Pandey. She also had to fetch water for his house. And, for this reason, from time to time the oven was not lit. She lived in the Pandit's village; therefore he had full authority to make her do any sort of odd job. In his opinion, if she received food for working from him, how could it be considered as work done without pay? He was doing her a favour, in fact, by letting her live in the village at all. It was spring and a day on which the fresh grain was fried and eaten and given as a gift. No fire was lit in the house.

Bhungi's oven was being put to good use today. There was a crowd worthy of a village fair around her. She had scarcely any opportunity to draw a breath.

Because of the impatience of the customers, **squabbles** kept breaking out. Then two servants arrived, each carrying a heaped basket of grain from Pandit Udaybhan with the order to parch it right away. When Bhungi saw the two baskets, she was alarmed. It was already after twelve and even by sunset, she would not have time to parch so much grain. Now, she would have to say at the parching oven until after dark for no payment. In despair, she took the two baskets. One of the **flunkeys** said menacingly, 'Don't waste any time or you'll be sorry.' With this command, the servants went away and Bhungi began to parch the grain.

It's no laughing matter to parch a whole maund of grain. She had to keep stopping from the parching in order to keep the oven fire going. So, by sundown not even half the work was done. She was afraid Panditji's men would be coming. She began to move her hands all the more frantically. Soon, the servants returned and said, 'Well, is the grain parched?' Feeling bold, Bhungi said, "Can't you see? I'm parching it now." "The whole day's gone and you haven't finished any more grain than this! Have you been roasting it or spoiling it? This is completely uncooked! How's it going to be used for food?

It's the ruin of us! You'll see what Panditji does to you for this." The result was that the same night the oven was dug up and Bhungi was left without a means of livelihood.

(i) For each word given below, choose the correct meaning (as used in the passage) from the options provided. [2]

(1) *squabbles* (line 19)
(a) battles (b) talking to someone (c) quarrels (d) debates

(2) *flunkeys* (line 24)
(a) puppeteers (b) home wreckers (c) employers (d) man servants

(ii) Which word in the passage means the opposite of the word 'daring'? [1]
(a) obliged (b) alarmed (c) afraid (d) parch

(iii) Answer the following questions briefly using your own words.
(a) How did Bhungi earn her livelihood? [2]
(b) Why was Pandit Udaybhan against paying Bhungi? [2]
(c) What does the author mean by "She had scarcely any opportunity to draw a breath"? [2]
(d) What did one of the servants of Pandit Udaybhan warn Bhungi about? [2]
(e) Which word in the passage shows that the old woman started working hastily in a disorderly manner out of anxiety? [1]

(iv) Describe the hard work and the plight of Bhungi in your own words not exceeding 50. [8]

Question 5.

SP-10

(i) Fill in each of the numbered blanks with the correct form of the word given in brackets. Do not copy the passage but write in correct serial order the word or phrase appropriate to the blank space. [4]

Example: The old priest ......(0)...... (ask) his congregration to stand up.

Answer (0) asked

The Singapore Botanical Garden, founded in 1859, is one of the leading tropical gardens in the world. It ...**(1)**... (attract) over twenty thousand visitors weekly. Some of these visitors ...**(2)**... (travel) from countries as far as France.

Besides ...**(3)**... (serve) as a public park, it ...**(4)**... (be) also a center for research on plant growth and improvement. Currently, some three thousand species of plants ...**(5)**... (flourish) in the garden. This collection ...**(6)**... (expand) through exchange and donations.

Tourists ...**(7)**... (visit) the garden can also ...**(8)**... (expect) to see several varieties of orchids, including our national flower.

(ii) Fill in each blank with appropriate words. [4]
(a) Japanese trains are almost always ...... time.
(b) The kid was so short that he couldn't see ...... the steering wheel.
(c) I waited for him .... 8:30 a.m. and then I left for the office alone.
(d) Can you prepare the dishes .... I fetch milk from the nearby store?

(e) I was ill .... a few days last week.

(f) There is someone ... the door. Go and check who it is.

(g) I didn't miss a single class ..... my first year.

(h) Would you like anything to drink ...... your meal?

(iii) Join the following sentences to make one complete sentence **without using and**, **but** or **so**. Choose the correct option. [4]

(1) There are no oranges in the shop. We have to buy bananas.
   (a) As there are no oranges in the shop, we have to buy bananas.
   (b) As there is no oranges in the shop, we have to buy bananas.
   (c) As there are no oranges in the shop, we had to buy bananas.
   (d) As there are no orange in the shop, we have to buy banana.

(2) He ran for the morning assembly. He was late.
   (a) He ran for the morning assembly as he is getting late.
   (b) He ran for the morning assembly because he was late.
   (c) He running for the morning assembly as he was getting late.
   (d) He run for the morning assembly as he got late.

(3) The pick pocket saw the policeman. He ran away at once.
   (a) As soon as the pick pocket saw the policeman, he run away.
   (b) As soon as the pick pocket sees the policeman, he runs away.
   (c) As soon as the pick pocket saw the policeman, he ran away.
   (d) As soon as the police saw the pick pocket, he ran away.

(4) Sunil is tall. Sanjay is taller.
   (a) Sunil is more tall than Sanjay.
   (b) Sanjay is more tall than Sunil.
   (c) Sunil is taller than Sanjay.
   (d) Sanjay is taller than Sunil.

(iv) Choose the correct option to rewrite the following according to the instructions given after each sentence. [8]

(1) As soon as the teacher went out of the class, the students started talking.
   [Begin with : No sooner....]
   (a) No sooner did the teacher go out of the class then the students started talking.
   (b) No sooner did the teacher went out of the class when the students started talking.
   (c) No sooner did the teacher go out of the class than the students started talking.
   (d) No sooner did the teacher goes out of the class than the students starts talking.

(2) It is too hot to go out.
   [Rewrite using : so ... that...]
   (a) It is so hot that we can go out.
   (b) It is so hot that we cannot go out.
   (c) It is so hot that we could not go out.
   (d) It is so hot that we should not go out.

(3) Do not go to sleep before I return from market.
   [Rewrite using : until]
   (a) Do not go to sleep until I returns from the market.
   (b) Do not go to sleep until I return from the market.
   (c) Do not go sleeping until I return from the market.
   (d) Do not go sleep until I return from the market.

(4) Sachin Tendulkar is the best batsman of the world.
   [Rewrite using the positive degree of adjective 'best']
   (a) No batsmen in the world is so good as Sachin Tendulkar.
   (b) No batsman in the world is so good to be like Sachin Tendulkar.

(c) No batsman in the world is as good as Sachin Tendulkar.
(d) No batsman in the world is good as Sachin Tendulkar.

(5) She was not certain about the trip.
[Use : decide]
(a) She wouldn't decide if she wanted to go to the trip.
(b) She wouldn't decide about the trip.
(c) She couldn't decide about the trip.
(d) She couldn't decide if she wanted to go to the trip.

(6) Airport authorities will inform you if the flight is delayed.
[Begin with : should.....]
(a) Should the flight delays, airport authorities will inform you.
(b) Should the flight delay, airport authorities will inform you.
(c) Should the flight be delayed, airport authorities will inform you.
(d) Should the flight is delayed, airport authorities will inform you.

(7) The walls would have been painted green by us.
[Rewrite using : Active Voice.....]
(a) We would paint the walls green.
(b) We would have painted the walls green.
(c) I would have painted the walls green.
(d) We should have painted the walls green.

(8) She said to me, 'I was waiting for my sister.'
[Rewrite using : Indirect speech]
(a) She told me that she had been waiting for her sister.
(b) She told me that she had been waiting for my sister.
(c) She told me that she was waiting for her sister.
(d) She told me that she was waiting for my sister.

For Answers scan QR code